Making & Flying

FIGHTER KITES

Making & Flying
FIGHTER KITES

Philippe Gallot

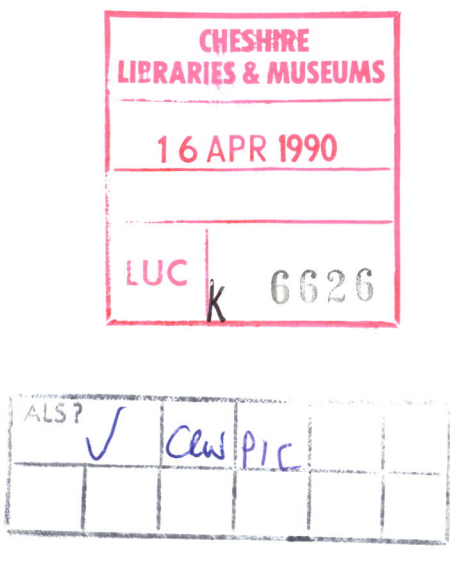
B. T. Batsford Ltd., London

ISBN 0 85219 807 8 (cased)

Typeset by Tradespools Ltd, Frome, Somerset
and printed in Great Britain by
Courier International, Tiptree, Essex

for the publishers
B. T. Batsford Ltd
4 Fitzhardinge Street
London W1H 0AH

Acknowledgements

I would like to thank my friends, the members of 'Le Cerf-Volant Club de France' for their everlasting encouragement to develop my designs.

A special thank you to Joel Theze and Martine Chatel, who organised a wonderful Fighter Kite festival in Angers (France), and to my friends at the Indian Embassy in Paris for sharing their flying and fighting technique.

A warm thank you to Eric Stempell, who has spent a lot of time perfecting my technical designs.

My thanks to my British friends for their support. Thank you to Tony Slater, Ludovic Petit, Martyn Lawrence and Takeshi Nishibayashi for their designs; to Chantal Barret for her special tricks for the construction of the fighters; to Jean Marie Gadonneix for his assistance in the painting and decoration of some models; to Michel Darnis and Philippe Albert Hesselmann for their photographs; and to Stephen Huffstutler and the International School of Paris for their computer assistance.

Finally, I would like to thank my dear wife for her many hours spent assisting me in the preparing of the manuscript, despite her not being a kite enthusiast.

Photographs by
Philippe-Albert Hesselmann
Eric Stempell
Michel Darnis
Martyn Lawrence
Philippe Gallot

Contents

Preface

It gives me great pleasure to introduce this informative and entertaining book by Philippe, who I first met at the International Kite Festival in Dieppe, France, in 1984.

We mad kite-flyers from England had crossed the Channel to join our French friends in a kite-flying bonanza.

Kite-flying is a healthy, enjoyable pastime, a sport brought to us from the East, which has given pleasure for hundreds of years and is increasing in popularity in Europe and the rest of the world. Many people make their own kites, and Philippe has written this book for those who wish to make their own Fighters.

In competition, kite-flyers try to bring their opponent's fighter down. Some of them use about 40 metres of 'Manjha' (line coated in powdered glass) so that when the pilots manoeuvre, the lines engage and some get cut.

Philippe's book is a must for all kite-flyers and an easy-to-read instruction for those taking up the sport.

Ron Moody
(Winner of several fighter kite competitions)

Introduction

You will have bought this book either because you already know about this type of kite or because you are very curious about it.

A lot of people know about kites, but very few are aware that fighter kites exist. I found out about this type of kite some years ago, and was very interested to build one and try it out. My first attempt was an Indian square: very simple to construct, and a good flyer.

I looked amongst the scanty information I had for the correct instructions to fly. No luck! So I went to the nearest field (in Paris, that is not easy to find) ... and I had a go. I could not start: the kite kept falling. A passer-by saw me and offered assistance, which I accepted with a smile. And off it went! I really enjoyed my first flight.

After a few flights, I started to be able to manoeuvre all over the sky. Two months later, I entered a competition, and was 'cut' in the first two seconds. Nevertheless, I met a good fighter pilot and we talked more than we flew. Since that day, I have spent a lot of my leisure time building and designing new models. I have also been involved with several competitions, and even won a few!

Flying fighter kites should be considered as a sport where skills, speed of eye, judgement and anticipation are practised during every second of your flight.

For you children, learning to fly these kites is a must. You will find it very enjoyable and challenging. In India, where lots of people fly fighter kites, the best pilots are often children. Furthermore, what a super way of spending a good afternoon, trying to cut your friend's line ... You can organise special competitions at school, with your neighbourhood or local clubs.

In order to have a good group of pilots, try to build one model in a group workshop. Parents can take part, helping you with the cutting of bamboo and gluing. Look through the book and decide which kite is the easiest to construct. (My advice would be to start with the Indian Square.)

1 *A young Indian man who made me a cutting line. Moulana Jamaludin is a very sharp fighter. His native knowledge and many hours of practice have made him a terrific pilot!*

Chapter 1
What is a fighter kite?

This question is often asked. Of course, the name itself indicates some kind of violence and aggression! This is not the case and certainly has nothing to do with kite-flying. A fighter kite is a piece of art, often home-made and decorated to embellish the sky. The fighter kite is a very fine machine which has the advantage that it can be driven in every direction, yet can be controlled to fly with extreme precision. Flying a fighter kite is, above all, a relaxing experience and a challenging reward to both the builder and the pilot.

The kites are small, can be made with all sorts of material and cost very little to build. It should not take more than one hour to make one to suit you. A fighter can be of several different shapes and sizes, but its most relevant distinguishing feature is that the bow is flexible. The kite itself is usually flat when at rest. The bow is the motor of the kite. When in action, the fighter kite moves in the desired direction, due, technically speaking, to the deformation of the bow. Once towed, the bow changes its shape. It becomes dihedral, which gives the kite a stability of flight path. The kite changes direction as soon as the bow returns to its rest position. Pull slightly on the line, and the kite goes in another direction. Flying a fighter is resumed by activating the bow in the correct way, by a constant traction and release of the flying line. A good balance between the length and the width of a kite makes it a fighter kite, but its speed is regulated by the strength of the bow. A soft bow will be fine for a light-wind slow fighter, while a strong bow will generate a very fast kite. I recommend that you build and experiment with both types.

The true fighter kite is designed to fly in combat, using a special type of line, with the object of trying to cut your opponent's line. These fighter competitions are well organized and have strict rules. It would be risky to get involved on your first test flight! A lot of practice and time is needed.

I fly fighter kites because they are a pleasure to drive around in the air. I play many games and spend most of my time enjoying the improvement of the art of being a good pilot.

All fighter kites are manipulated in the same way. Once you have mastered flying one, you are qualified to try any other type.

Do not be put off by the name, but rather build your own and go and enjoy yourself. I promise you, you will not be disappointed!

Chapter 2
Building a fighter kite

Tools

To build fighter kites, you will need a few tools:

- a saw
- a ruler
- a pair of scissors
- a cutter
- a strong sharp knife
- a hammer
- pens and pencils
- a tape measure
- some clips or clothes pegs
- a compass to draw circles
- a wood plane
- a board to lay down your work

2 *Tools for making fighter kites*

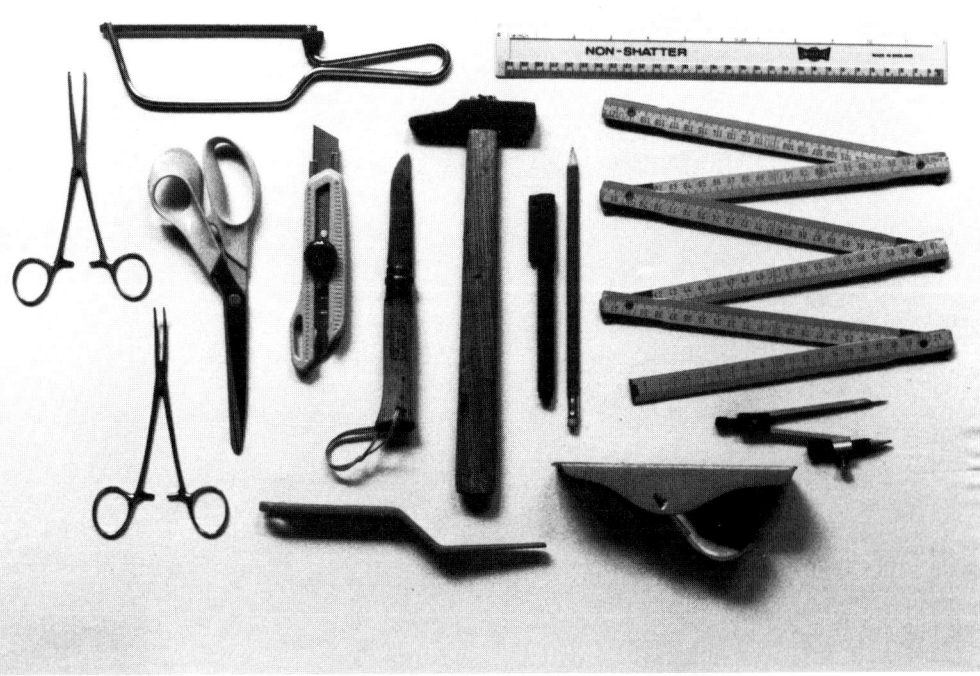

The following are also needed:
- different types of glue (both clear and contact types)
- several sizes, colours and types of tape
- fibreglass rods of different diameters
- string
- needles
- a pair of cutting pliers
- bamboo sticks
- cotton thread

3 *Materials for making fighter kites*

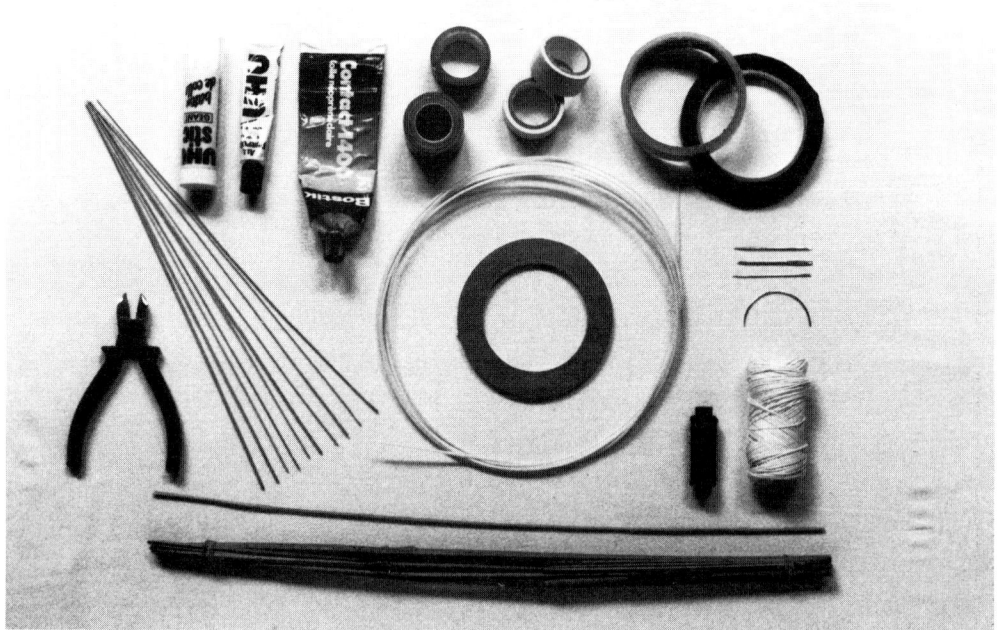

Materials

Several types of material can be used to build a fighter kite. Each one has its own characteristics. Look for the type which will be best for the design you are going to build. The quality of the cover is important. It would be a mistake to build only paper fighter kites: you might regret it when the grass is damp! A strong-pulling fighter will have a short life if made of paper, while the same model made of nylon or plastic could last many years. The choice of cover also depends on the kind of decoration you intend to use. Test your cover material before making your final decision.

A fighter kite can be built with:
- plastic bag
- Mylar
- nylon
- hard Tyvek
- soft Tyvek
- tissue paper
- newspaper
- book cover plastic
- greaseproof paper

4 *Several types of plastic suitable for kitemaking*

Soft Tyvek and nylon can be sewn and glued with the appropriate glue, while the other materials should be sealed or taped as well as being glued. Plastic and nylon do not take paint very well, but some types of plastic will take felt-pens and coloured inks. Remember to do your tests for glue and colours before starting to build!

Working with bamboo

In this chapter, I would like to give some advice regarding the use of bamboo in the construction of fighter kites.

In non-kite-builders' minds, bamboo is just a stick for use with garden plants. Well, this is just about right, because it is in a garden centre or a big store that you will find the bamboo sticks you need. You may have some difficulty finding the exact piece of bamboo that suits your construction. Don't worry! You will create the shape you need by trimming and splitting. When buying bamboo rods, look for a big diameter. Remember that you would never use a whole rod, no matter what size you wish to build.

Once you have chosen your rod, you can start working on the sticks. The bow for a fighter kite is made from a strip of rod. Adults are strongly advised to supervise children during this process.

Take a sharp knife and split the rod in half from top to bottom. You may have two uneven pieces: this is not unusual. Remove the inside knots. The next exercise will be much easier to do. Estimate the thickness of the sticks you need. Take on half of the rod, and split it again from top to bottom. Your rough stick is now taking shape. In order to produce a good bow, look for a thick bamboo core.

Measure the length of stick needed and add a little extra which will be removed once the stick is fixed on the kite (this makes holding easier). To scrape my sticks I use a wood shaver. Bamboo is a very hard material and makes a lot of fine splinters, so be extra careful with your fingers. You may find it easier to wear a glove to hold the stick.

Scrape the stick from the middle towards the tips. Sometimes the bamboo is easier to scrape on one side than on the other. Work on both sides at the same time. Never work on the outside skin, the glossy part of the bamboo. Keep testing the flexibility while sanding down. The blade of a good sharp knife is very useful for scraping the two sides. The profile of both the central stick and the bow should be triangular. This shape is not essential, but it really gives an extra 'boost'. You will find that your first attempts are not up to your expectations, but with practice you will become a bamboo champion!

Trim your bow finer for a small kite than for a bigger fighter. The type of wind you expect to play with is also an important consideration when designing the sticks. You may wish to have two kites of the same type, but built for different wind forces. There is nothing more frustrating than going on to a field with a kite that won't fly!

When positioning the bow on the kite, put the glossy part towards the top. For the central stick the glossy side of the bamboo is glued to the kite cover, except when building a foldable fighter.

When embarking upon a stick-splitting session, take the opportunity to prepare some extra ones for future kites or for repairs. I always have some bows and central sticks ready in case of an unexpected breakage. On the field, you will need some good tape for running repairs in order to finish a good flying session. Once back home, review your provisional repairs!

Bits and pieces

Many different gadgets can be used to create your own kite. It is advisable to look in junk shops for odds and ends. I often wander around jumble sales, market places, superstores, ironmongers, charity shops, angling shops, wood merchants, and other places where I may find something which will suit the kite I have in mind! Haberdashery departments are a must for a visit. Once acquired, keep your treasures in a specially designed box. They may be useful another day!

Keep some metal cans for constructing spools. Pieces of plywood of various dimensions and thicknesses are also very valuable.

A very useful trick is to attach a bead to the centre of the kite, through which you can thread the bow. This allows the kite to be folded and carried. At the tips of each wing a small aluminium tube of a slightly bigger diameter than the bow is attached to house the end of the bow, so that it can be removed when travelling or allow you to change the strength by fixing a double bow. Adhesive tape will secure the tube to the cover. Some kite-flyers prefer to have kites that cannot be dismantled. I am one of them. In this case, you need to have a big box to carry and store your kites when going to the flying field. Often it will save your kites from being walked upon. A special compartment in your box could be reserved for the storage of spools and spare lines as well as a repair kit. Ready-prepared bows, to replace broken ones and to change to suit stronger or even much lighter winds are most welcome! During festivals, I find it very rewarding to have prepared spare covers for my favourite kites, which means they take a very short time to repair ready for a new flight.

For group kitebuilding workshops, you may wish to make a pattern (template) with thick cardboard. It will be easier to draw around the shape than to measure each part. You may wish to do this even if you are only making a few kites. It will save you time and frustration should you need to make the same kite again. Think of your friends and other envious onlookers.

Chapter 3
Pictorial guide to building a fighter kite

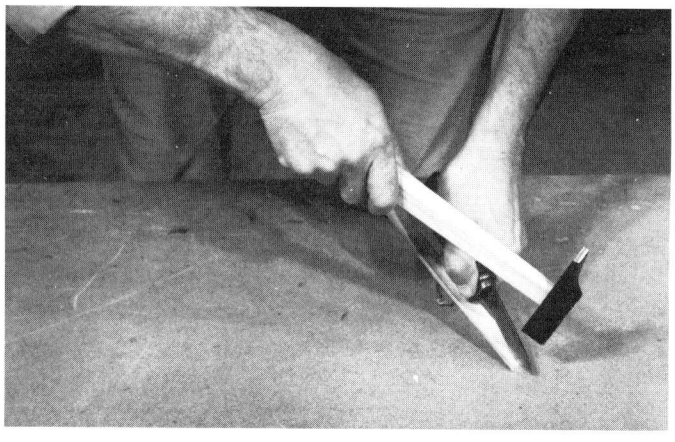

5 *Once you have split a big rod of bamboo with a sharp tool, take the piece that will be suitable for your stick (spine or bow)*

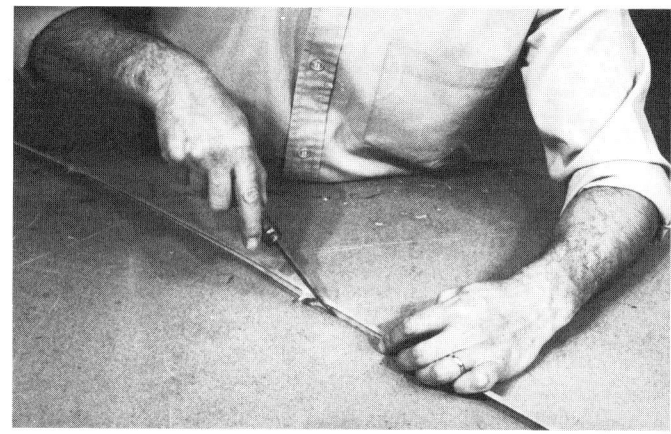

6 *With the knife, remove the knots from the split rod*

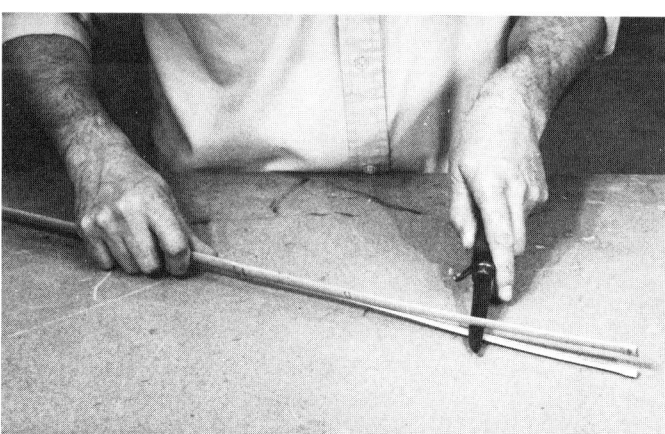

7 *Using a knife and a hammer, split the remaining thickness of bamboo. Go from one end to the other. You may find that the knife will not go as straight as expected (this is usual for our local bamboo rods)*

8 *Split your stick to the approximate thickness*

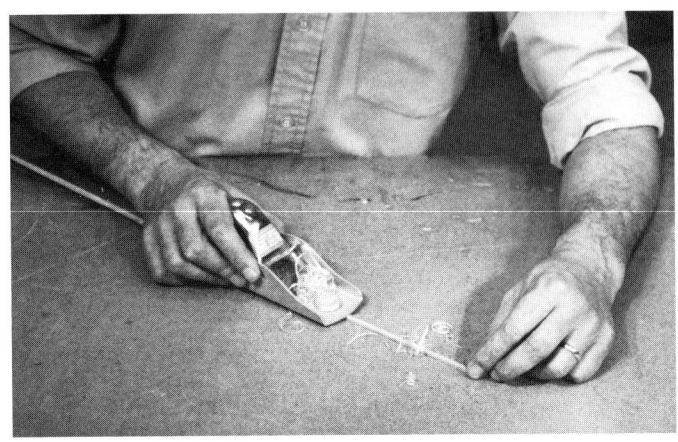

9 *Start shaving the stick with a wood shaver in order to reduce the thickness and get your stick into shape*

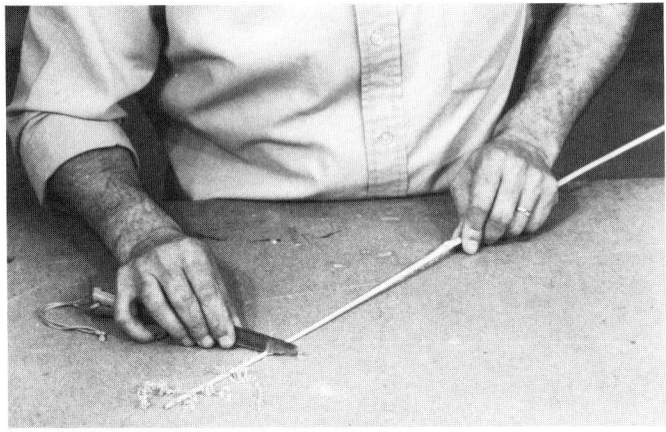

10 *Scrape the stick with a blade. Here, the stick is almost trimmed to shape*

11 *Give a finishing touch to the stick using sandpaper*

12 *Measure and cut your stick*

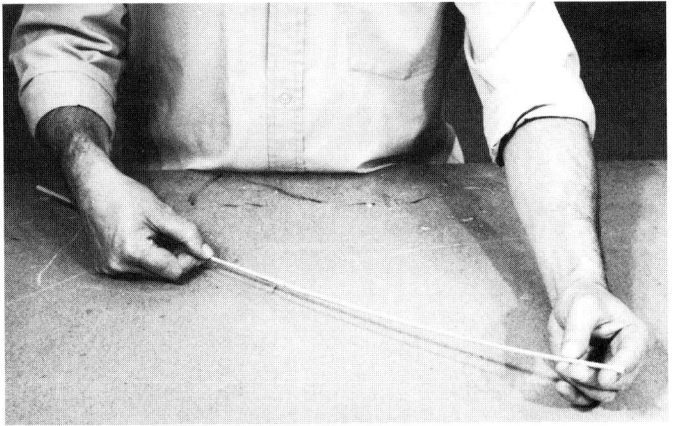

13 *The finished stick. If you are making a spine, test the flexibility. For a bow, do not forget to trim the tips of the stick and see if the flexibility is sufficient*

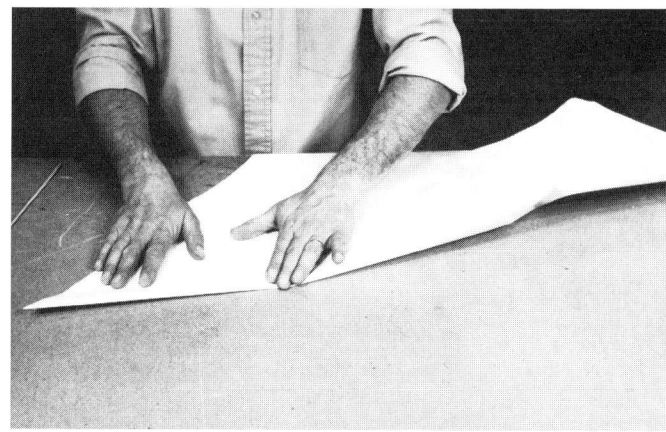

14, 15 *After choosing the material with which you wish to build your kite, fold in half in order to have a perfect axis of symmetry*

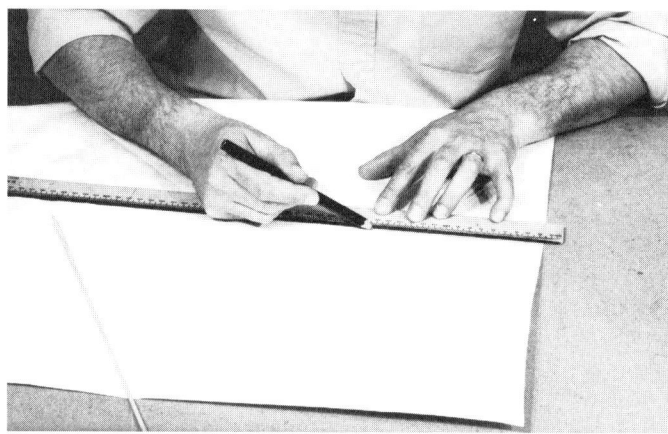

16 *Draw the outside lines of your model on to the chosen cover*

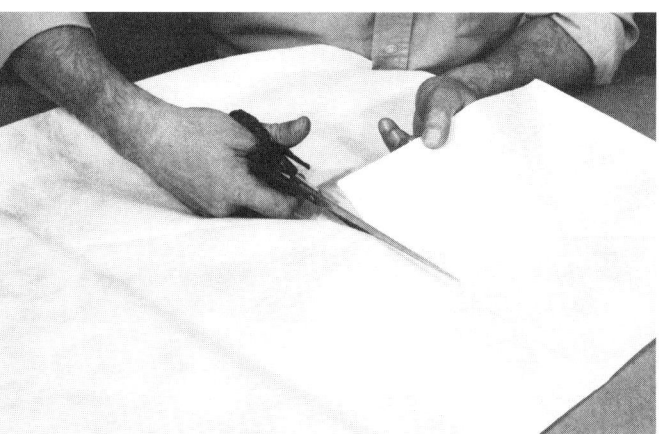

17 *Cut your shape. Do not forget any extra pieces for the folds over the wings*

18 *Lay a coat of contact glue exactly over the axis of the kite*

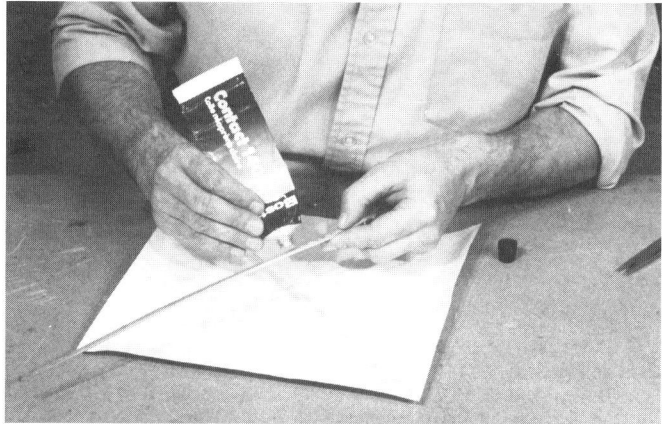

19 *While the glue grows tacky, put a coat on the glossy side of the stick*

20 *When the glue no longer sticks to your finger, lay the stick down. Be careful: you can only do this once when using contact glue! Press hard to make sure the contact is firm*

21 *Cut two small pieces of the same material, and reinforce both the front and the tail of the kite*

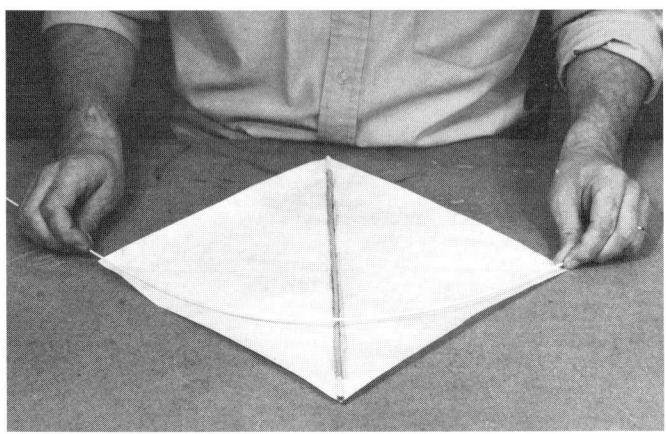

22 *Measure the length of the material needed for the bow (here, I am using a fibreglass bow)*

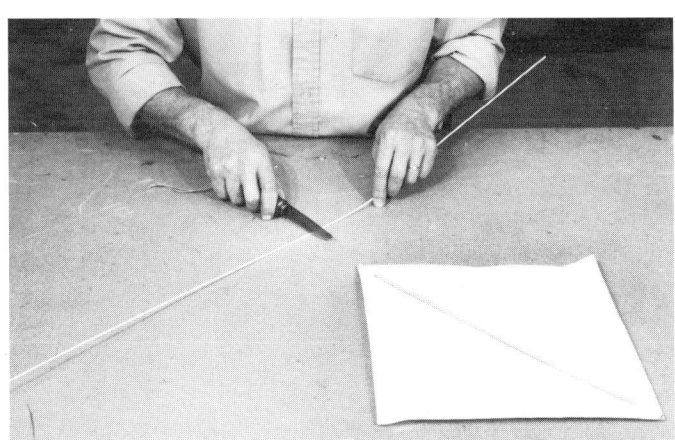

23 *Cut the exact length for the bow*

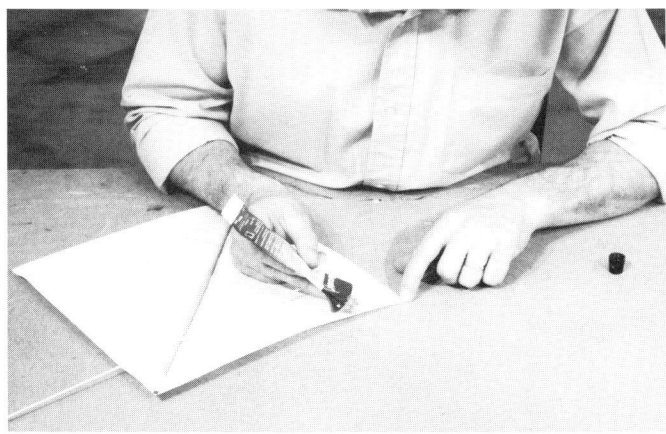

24 *Put some glue on the cover which will be folded over the tips of the bow. Make sure you have marked the correct length to be glued*

25 *Place one end of the bow over the glue and fold over the tip. Press hard*

26 *Using a clip to maintain the first side which has been glued, lay some glue on the other side of the wing so that it will be ready to take the other tip of the bow*

27 *Glue and fold over the tip of the bow. Use another clip to keep the bow in place while the glue is setting. Prepare the little pieces of material to reinforce the kite where you will punch the cover for the bridle*

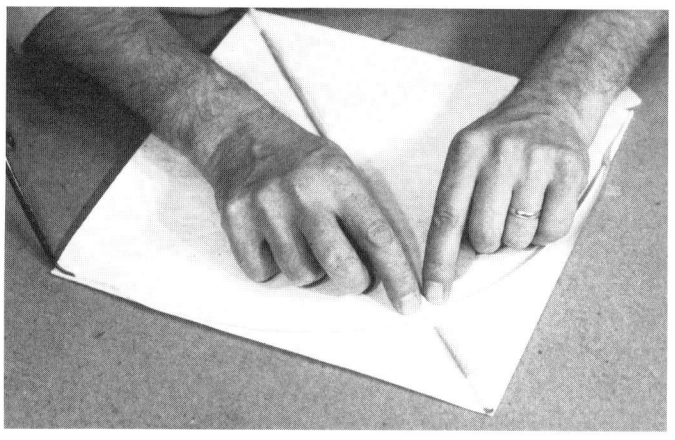

28 *The small piece of extra material is glued over the spine at the level of the upper bridle attachment. Do the same for the lower bridle*

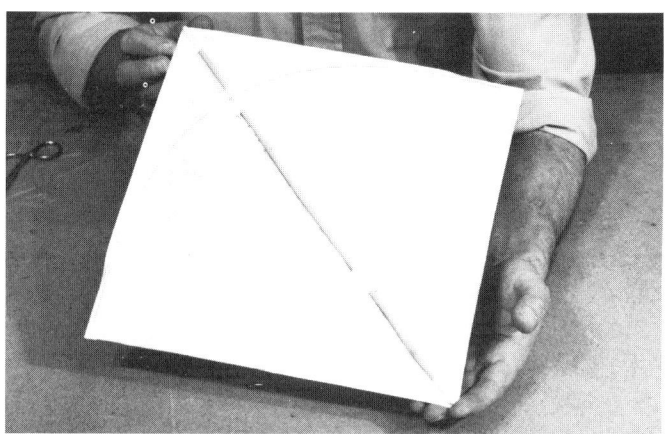

29 *Your kite cover is finished, but you still need to make the bridle system*

30 *Decorate your model using paint, felt-tip pens or ink*

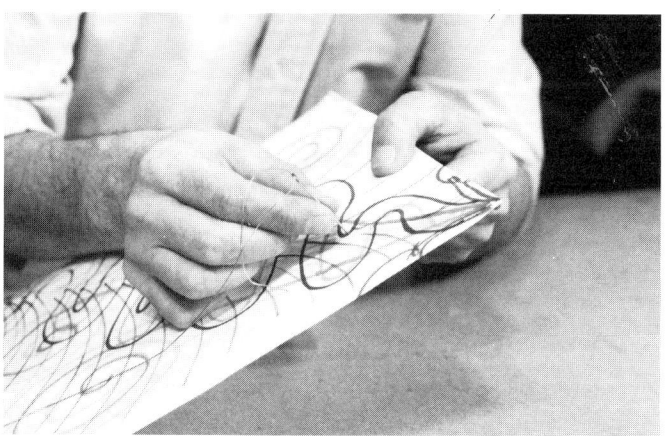

31 *Cut a much longer piece of string than needed to make your bridle. With a needle, pierce the cover from the side which will be facing you once the kite is flying. Be certain to punch the hole as close as possible to the spine and the bow*

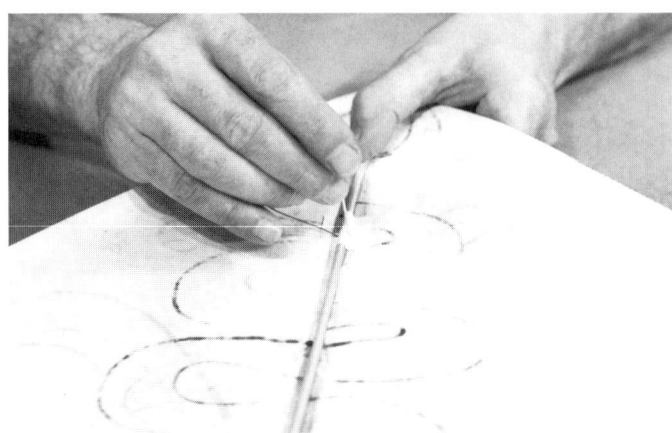

32 *Once the string has gone through the cover, make two turns around the bow and pierce through the cover again, making sure that the needle goes through the other side of the spine*

33 *Do the same for the back of the kite. Pierce through the cover and come back with the needle on the other side of the spine*

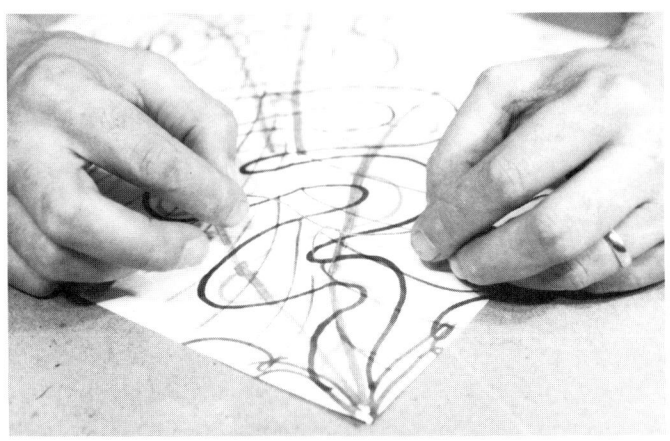

34, 35 *Make the knots, leaving a small piece for the fine tuning adjustment*

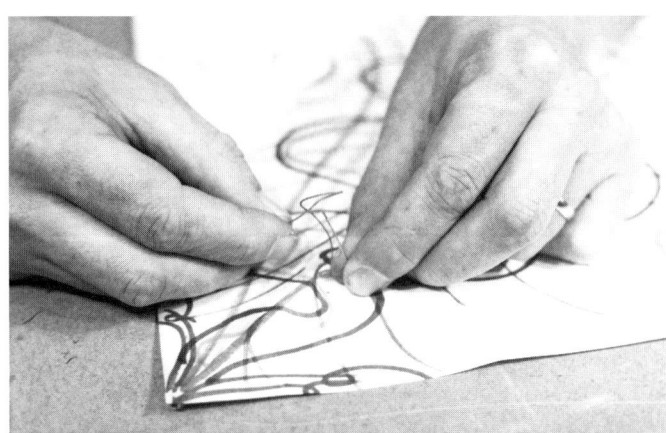

36 *To do the fine tuning, make a small loop with the bridle string and insert the little extra piece left over inside the loop. This will reduce the length of the bridle and give you a better tuning. This should only be done on the flying field*

37 *Once the fine tuning is done correctly, you can finish off the towing knot by making a double loop. If you measure the bridle lengths before making the final knot, you may have a well tuned kite right away*

38, 39 *Fix the towing knot to the flying line. You may either make a knot or a twisted loop. Furthermore, a small swivel is ideal for quick starts*

Chapter 4
Flying fighter kites

Before flying a kite, you should be aware of some safety rules. Never fly when:
- thunder is on the way
- near electric lines
- amongst people
- near trees
- near railway lines
- near airports
- near roads
- near farmland with animals

Always anticipate a failure and the need for a quick recovery!

Now, you are ready for the much needed instructions. Of course, it is easier to learn with an established pilot! I will try my best to help you.

By now you should have at least one fighter kite and a spool with non-cutting line. Get someone to help you for the start. You must warn your helper to move back away from the take-off point. You may expect to do a good job, but always anticipate what might happen.

Your kite should be attached to the line. Let go 20–30 metres (65–98 feet) of line, keeping it stretched but not tight. When you are ready, signal your helper to release the kite towards the sky. At this moment, you should move back too, so that your kite clears your assistant.

If your bridle is correctly set, the kite will go straight up into the sky. If the kite spins, pull on the line slightly or take some back. This should adjust the flight. If it does not help, you must adjust the bridle. It is either too short at the back or too long at the front. Finally, if your kite is still spinning, then you may have an unbalanced weight on the wings. Add some weight to the lighter side until the kite is perfectly balanced on the centre stick. The final cause of disturbance to a good take-off could be that you have made your bow too stiff and so the elasticity is not the same on both sides.

During test flights, you will often find that small adjustments need to be made. Do not let this rob you of your enthusiasm: it happens to me as well!

The area of flying can also have some effect on tuning a good kite.

I went several times to a famous place in Paris, where many kite flyers practise. Even though I knew that my new kite was well made, I just could not get it

40 *Joe Vaughan from the USA is giving a lesson to a newcomer to fighter kites. Using his expertise in flying Grandmaster Fighter Kites, Joe has successfully trained his 'student' in no more than five minutes*

41 *Felix Mottram from England has just been caught . . . His sharp manipulation will make him win this splendid fight. Even Paul and Helen (on the right) didn't believe it possible for Felix to come out alive!*

to go! I often see that, at low altitude, the wind disturbance is just impossible. A kite-flyer should have some knowledge about wind and the landscape effects. Studying the weather forecast can help a great deal. If you go to school, ask your science teacher for some details. If you want more detailed information, go to your local library and take out some books about glider and delta plane flying. Most of these have chapters on weather observations and analyses of the best clouds and draught spots.

You must remember that you are flying a very special type of kite which

42 *A young French boy makes his first test flight with one of Joe Vaughan's fighters. A small tail has been attached to reduce the speed of the kite and help the beginner to control his machine*

43 *Our famous master, Ron Moody from England, has engaged his kite in a fight with a member of the Indian team . . . looking at Ron's smile, I bet he has caught his opponent!*

requires a certain amount of practice and manipulation. So let us imagine that you have a perfect kite and the right wind. Once your kite has taken off, and you have moved away from your assistant, your nerves may start to go! Yes, you are now in full control of your machine. Keep it flying high for safety and a good practice.

Remember that in fighter kite flights you should never pull on the line if the kite takes a dive. As you will know, the kite is directional once the line is in traction, and so you will crash. If you are in a diving situation and want to recover from it, just *let go the line* slightly. Your machine will take a turn and escape a horrible end! At this moment, give a very fine pull on the line and you will be safely back in the sky. This should be one of your first experiments in controlling the flight. Try it: do not forget to take your escape far enough above the ground.

After a few tries, you will have mastered the control of the kite and will be ready to experiment really close to the ground. Do remember that the ground wind may not be as stable as the one in altitude and that this will affect the stability of your flight.

A good fighter should respond to a slight pull or release of the line. To make the kite turn on its gravity point, let go the line and it will start to spin on its axis. To make it go in the direction you have chosen (it may not at your first attempt) pull the line a little to come out of the spin. The kite will then go in the direction its nose is pointed. Let go again, and it will spin and change direction.

A pilot should always handle the control line with a gentle touch. When you begin experimenting, you must adjust the bridle to a beginner's touch. Once you have a good control, re-adjust the bridle, making it more sensitive and fine for a delightful flight. I often re-adjust the bridle for my son so that he can get a correct flight control and enjoy his flying time without frustration.

The art of achieving a good balance and quick speed turns, dives and attacks is

44 *All the secrets are in the right hand . . . Ron Schroder from Holland is tuning one of his latest fighter kites. The nose of his kite is equipped with three pins. Ron is challenging a big kite which is towing several balloons*

45 *Jacob Twyford from England is giving a fine pull to cut his opponent's line. Jacob is testing one of the author's latest models. Admire the way he is concentrating on his flight*

a mixture of the setting of different adjustments. Of course, the weather conditions have a lot to do with the setting and sensitivity of the kite. I often compare flying fighters to fly-fishing: it is all a matter of handling the line.

Line manipulation is also very important. You should never hold it tight nor attach it to your hand. Your finger control lets you give or take as freely as possible.

In competition fights, you will always see two people in charge of one kite: the pilot, who controls the fighter, and his assistant, who takes care of the spool and of feeding the line to the pilot, as well as of the recovery of the line back to the spool. The role of the assistant is crucial. His manipulation must be exactly in accordance with the pilot. A slight mistake from the assistant could cause a fatal error from which the pilot could not recover. I remember once, during a competition in Dieppe, having asked for an assistant to help me with the spool during a set fight. I have to forgive this good friend, but he was the cause of my defeat! I needed a few feet of line in order to escape an attack and take a very sharp dive under my opponent, (he would have been caught and cut), but my assistant was holding the spool too tight, so that when I pulled some line, I snatched it and let go of my kite. 'Quelle horreur'! There was no escape: I had lost the fight!

I find that children enjoy being responsible for the spool as much as flying. It is a good way of learning to become a pilot, just as in golf, being the caddie often helps to judge the game.

This little story shows also the importance of a round spool, as the handle of the spool runs in your hand like a wheel trapped in wheel bearings.

Study the drawings carefully so that you have the right picture of your needs. It will be too late to refer to the instruction manual once your fighter kite is in the air!

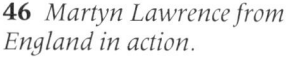

46 *Martyn Lawrence from England in action.*

Chapter 5
Fighter kite line

As you will see in this book, most of the kites are rather small in size. If you study the history of fighter kites, you will find that there were some very large fighters which were manipulated by several assistants. I will not discuss these here, as many authors have already developed the subject.

The line for fighter kites can be of various types. Of course you should look for a fairly strong line, but it must not be too strong. The task is to find the line that will suit your own needs. The ideal line is one that can take your kite in the air yet withstand the necessary efforts during stronger pulls and dives. You will need to experiment with several types of strength before flying. Do not forget that too strong a line will also affect the flight, as the weight and friction of the line in the air will have some dragging effect.

47 *Several spools of different sizes, loaded with cutting and practice lines. All these spools are homemade. Each one carries a special line of a different thickness and strength*

When you start flying fighter kites, I recommend that you use cotton line with a breaking strength of about 3kg to 5kg (6-10lb). You must realise that the line is the life and the motor of your kite. I have lost kites because I had underestimated the strength of the line. It will never break at the time nor the length you expect!

Nylon line is not ideal. It will stretch and, futhermore, could hurt you badly. A really good line must be fine but never elastic. The kite is under control whenever you manipulate the line. Therefore nylon, or any line that will stretch, will not give the correct command to the kite.

When I am flying for practice I often choose a line to suit my fingers rather than my kite! It may really be a little too heavy, but it feels nice in the hand and gives a good 'feeling' about the kite.

A fighter kite pilot never wears gloves to control the line, even when flying with a cutting line. The cutting line, a very strange concept for a newcomer, is a must when entering a competition. The only cutting line that I know of is the Indian type, made of fine cotton line covered with glass powder. It is extremely sharp and, of course, cuts like a weapon. The friction of a cutting line on any other type of line will have the same result as if you use a razor blade!

Never let children play with this type of line unless they are supervised and good fighters. You should also remove the cutting line when flying amongst other, non-fighter, kites, otherwise you will become very unpopular because of the damage you will cause. When we fly for shows and in front of spectators, we always warn about the danger of this type of line. During competitions, fighters cover their fingers with tape to avoid severe finger cuts.

In India, a fighter kite pilot prepares his own cutting line. I have never made one myself, but I do use ready-made line when going for a show. I will discuss some fighting strategies in the chapter on playing and having real fights.

In my kite case I carry several types of spools with different lines. This allows other pilots to play, and means I have the right line for any type of kite and weather conditions.

The cutting line should not get wet: the cotton becomes soft and the glass powder comes off the line. If you have no choice, and you must fly on a wet day, you must protect your spool with some kind of cover. The cutting line is usually in the air during dry days. After a few fights, the pilot cuts off the piece that he has been using, because the running of the line through the fingers lessens the quantity of the glass powder and will make that piece of line too smooth for the next fight.

I have seen other types of cutting line which actually carry several razor blades; also a star-shaped cutting device attached at some point on the line. A friend of mine has tried using twisted kevlar and very fine metal wire. Personally, I do not like to fly with anything other than Indian cutting line. I must insist on the awareness of safety rules, both when using these lines and when experimenting.

The best, and probably the cheapest, line one could use is a good button thread, which can be found almost in every big store. When you look for your cotton line ask to try the breaking strength on a short piece. The line should break before it hurts your hand. I am known in several shops in Paris for fiddling with cotton spools and breaking the line! You will certainly get some remarks and be asked why you are doing this: be prepared with your answers! Finally, when flying try to avoid using twisted and knotted pieces of line. Any previously damaged part must be removed.

Chapter 6
Spools

There are several types of spool suitable for fighter kites. Nevertheless those you make yourself are the best, simply because you have designed them the way you feel is best suited to your needs. I like mine to have a long shaft, as this makes them much easier to handle.

The most important quality of a good spool is to pay out the line as quickly as possible without any friction. My long shaft one allows me to hold the spool with both hands when delivering the line. A well-balanced spool is crucial in order to give speed and good recovery of the feeding line. I have been given an old original weaving spool made of wood. This is my favourite spool because it has a lot of 'body weight'. A really good spool should be heavy and easy to spin. From a technical point of view, the greater the mass, the better the rotation of the spool. Rotation is accelerated with the weight, like a type of fly wheel.

You may not be as lucky as I am, and therefore should look for a good cylinder to create your spinning wheel. It must have some weight. If you use plywood or plastic pipe, then you must add some kind of material that will add ballast. Plaster, concrete, lead, steel or sand are all suitable materials.

I have given instructions for two different types of spool. I must say that a fighter kite does not work well without a spinning spool. You must forget right away any kind of spool not of a cylindrical type.

First, look for a good 'body weight' piece of heavy wood. The diameter may vary. A good diameter is 10cm or more. The bigger the diameter, the faster you will deliver or rewind the line. The correct weight of the 'body' of a spool should be 0·25kg (8oz) or more. With experience, you will find it very pleasant to manoeuvre the line with a heavy spool. This applies to fighter kites of at least 60cm (24in) span. For smaller kites, you do not need such a powerful spool.

If you refer to the chapter on flying, you will see that in fact you are very lucky, because whatever the spool weight is, it won't bother you too much, as it will be your assistant who holds it! Remember that you are the pilot and you need a sharp assistant (and a very enthusiastic one too!).

Otherwise, plant your spool into the ground with the shaft in the direction of the flight. If your spool is well made, the line will come out without difficulty.

In India they use a very special spool covered with cutting line. It is so well balanced that you can spin it with the tips of your fingers. It can deliver and

48 49 50 *A member of the Indian team fixing the bridle on one of his homemade big Indian paper fighter kites. This shows another way of getting the knots ready to take the bridle before being secured to the towing line*

recover the line at great speed. This technique is not as easy as it looks but, with time, you will be able to do a good job. The process is to let go the spool, and with a slight jump in the tips of the fingers give a spinning movement forward or backward, using the thumb as a safety edge to allow further spin without the spool falling off. The spool seems to cover a circular shape inside your fingers. The heavy, balanced rotation gives the effect of speed to recover or deliver the line. Please give this movement plenty of practice. I find it difficult, even after many years.

Often you will find that it is easier to recover a line laid on the ground than a stretched line in the sky with an uncontrollable kite flying all over the clouds: to practise your spinning, put the line out on the ground and start spinning towards the kite. Walk forward as the line goes around your spool.

When you fly by yourself, you will find that putting the line on the ground before take-off will enable you to get the kite in the air without having to deal with the spool.

My idea of using a shaft with one longer side helps a great deal because it allows you to control the take-off with the spool in both your hands. During competitions, several kite-fighters have asked me the reason for this long shaft. Never give your secret away, as you may lose your fight.

51 52 *Two spools with cutting lines. Notice the way each pilot is holding his spool. In Fig 52 the pilot is letting loose the line in order to escape his opponent*

The Korean spool is of a different shape. The system is similar ... I often get my sleeves caught in the shaft!

The second type of spool is made from an empty metal can. Drill a central hole through the can and glue in a wooden shaft (handle). Before inserting the shaft, fill the can with sand. Two wooden plywood discs of a larger diameter than the can are glued to both ends. This will stop the string rolling off the spool.

Remember that your spool is a very important factor in a good flight and needs to be seen as a principal part of a successful construction for winning flights. Take great care to design the correct one. (Some people use a fishing spinning wheel. I have never tried it.)

Finally, to avoid the line becoming entangled, use a cylindrical spool with a swivel to allow the line to spin freely when your fighter kite has been twisted round and round. It will stop your line getting in a mess. You can find these articles at your local angling centre.

Construction details

The long shaft spool

1) Make two discs of 15cm (6in) diameter from a piece of 5mm ($^3/_{16}$in) thick plywood (A).
2) Choose a shaft: a rod 1·5cm ($^5/_8$in) in diameter will do well (B).
3) Take an empty can or other type of cylindrical object. (C) Drill a hole in both ends to allow the shaft to go through.
4) Drill a hole of the same diameter in the two plywood discs. Push the rod into the first disc, followed by the cylinder which will be glued to the disc. Lay some glue on the second disc and insert it into the other side of the shaft.
5) Make sure that you have left enough room for your hand on the shorter side of the shaft. Assemble the entire construction, let it dry and decorate it using varnish or paint. The longer length of the shaft is trimmed to a pointed end (D)to enable the spool to be planted into the ground when flying your kite.
6) Choose a kind of line that will suit you and do not forget to make a strong knot on the spool before starting to roll the line on.
7) I often plant my spool behind me and draw the line between my legs.

If you wish to make another type of short shaft spool, just reduce the length of the rod!

53 *Construction diagram for the spool*

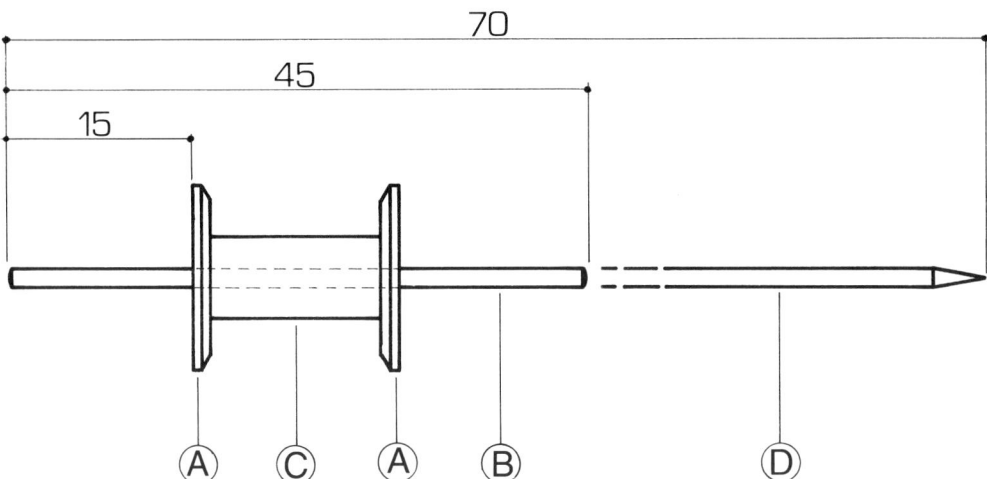

The big spool

1) Make two discs of plywood 1cm ($^3/_8$in) thick and 17cm (6$^3/_4$in)in diameter (A).
2) Draw another circle of 15cm (6in) diameter and using the radius, mark the diameter into six equal parts. You will need to do this on both discs. The marks made on the 15cm (6in) circle are the points where you will drill the holes for the sticks which join the two sections of the spool. I would suggest that you drill both discs at the same time. This will help to get a good fitting for the sticks.
3) Both discs should be trimmed on the inside to allow an easy run for the string. Before drilling your holes, make sure that you have the right measurement for the sticks: 20cm (8in) seems to be a good size. The two discs should already have been drilled to let the shaft (B) through.

4) Put some glue in the six holes and on one side of the sticks. Insert the shaft and plunge the sticks into the holes (C).
5) You are now ready to do the same on the other side of the spool. Leave enough room for your hands to hold the spool.
6) Once the spool is dry, give it a little touch with sandpaper and trim one end of the shaft.
7) Remember that you will leave the spool in the ground. You must therefore protect it with some paint or varnish. The decoration of the two discs is part of a good fighter kite show.

54 *The big spool*

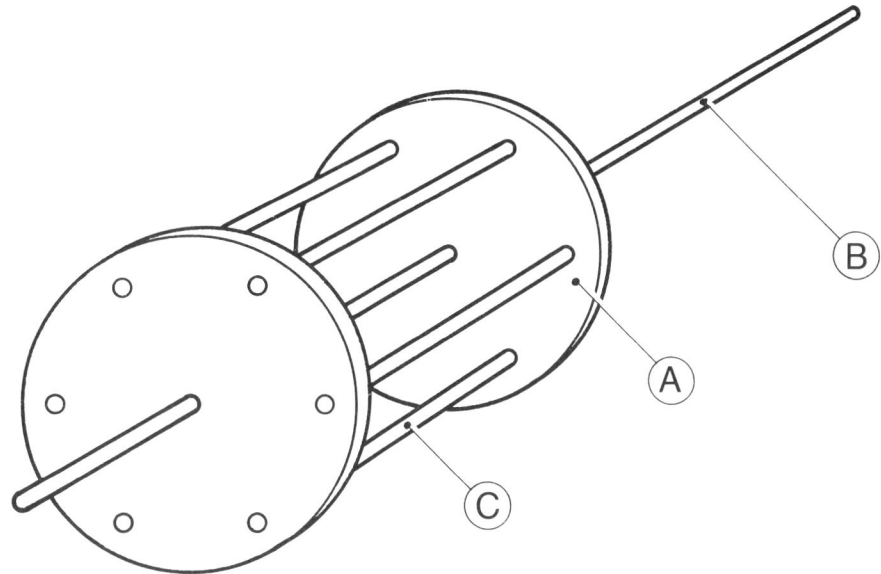

55 *The big spool, showing the position of holes in the disc*

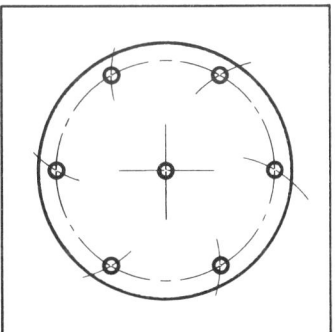

Chapter 7
Setting the bridle

The bridle is the string which is attached to the kite and is set in order to maintain the kite at the correct angle facing the wind. Fixing the bridle to the kite is as important as attaching a propeller to a helicopter! Be very careful.

The strength of the string used for the bridle should never be less than the flying line. Use a cotton thread. A needle is very handy to get the string through the cover without making a huge hole.

Most fighter kites have a two-leg bridle system. You will see in this book some with a three-leg and some with a four-leg bridle system. Nevertheless, the upper point of the bridle is always either on the exact junction of the central stick and the bow, or on both sides of the central stick but attached to the bow. The lower bridle is attached somewhere below half of the length of the central stick and the tail part of the kite. Very few fighters have the bridle set at the very end of the kite.

Once the bridle string is in the correct place and has been threaded through the cover, make a knot at the upper leg. You must leave an extra piece of string after the knot is made. This little extra piece is the fine tuning gadget. Next, adjust the lower bridle leg, leaving extra string before making the final knot on the central stick. Do the same again, leaving the little extra piece for fine tuning.

If you hold the kite by the bridle, it should be perfectly balanced on the axis of flight. Once this is done, the bridle towing-knot can be tied. Take both strings in your hand. Without letting the string get loose, measure the upper length by placing the string on the fixing point on the bow. Your upper bridle is now correctly adjusted. If you wish to give some extra body to the kite, allow 1cm ($^3/_8$in) extra above the bow junction. Still holding the two strings together, move both pieces until they are 1cm short of the lower knot.

Your kite is almost ready for the test: the last thing to do is to make a knot at the exact junction of both adjustments. Once you have made the towing knot, try to see if the kite is still well balanced and almost flat. A slight upwards angle of the nose will make the kite faster.

The final setting and the fine tuning can only be done on the flying ground. Remember the little extra pieces of string that we left at both bridle points? Well, you will now appreciate the fine tuning. If the kite goes in a series of continuous spins, it is too 'sharp' to the wind. Reduce the length at the back by

56a 56b *Two pilots adjusting the bridle and working on fine line tuning before getting ready to fight. The fine tuning is done to match the speed and condition of the wind.*

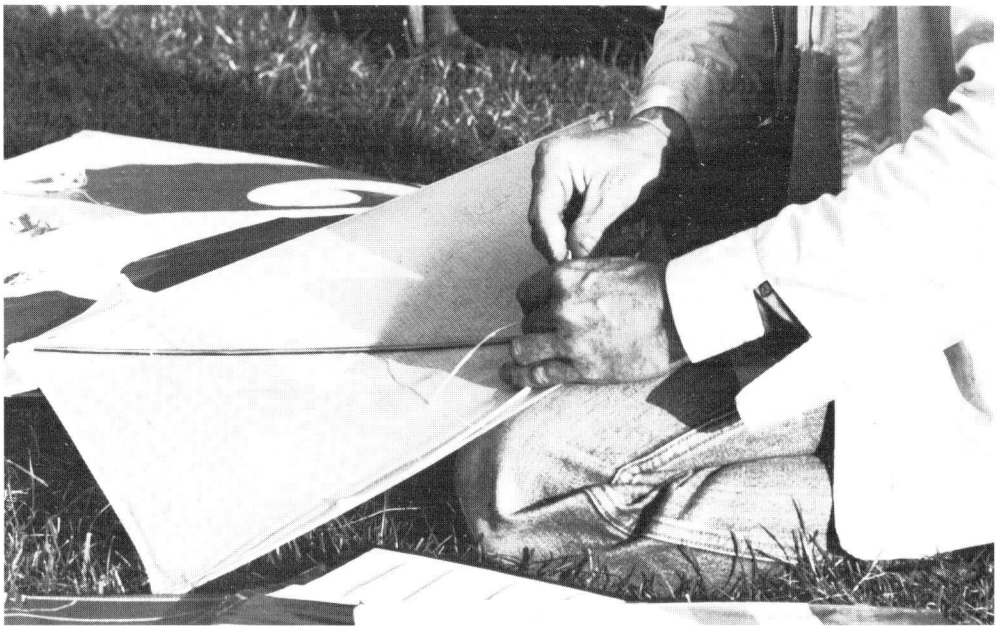

looping the lower bridle with that little piece of string. It will make the kite flatter to the wind. You could also give more bridle length from the front knot, but this is not so easy because the knot on the bow has been tightened. If the kite refuses to take off or seems to be very slow, adjust the front bridle to reduce the length. Once more, that little extra piece of string will be used to loop around and make a fine tuning. If you are a fan of fast moving fighters, tune the bridle to make the kite very unstable and a fast spinner. (The bridle will be shorter.)

With practice, the bridle tuning can be readjusted. Try several times before being sure of the final tuning. I have sometimes been unable to tune kites for several flights simply because the wind condition was not right. A lot of ground disturbance could make you think that you have built a bad kite. This is *not true*! Just try again another day.

Chapter 8
Designs

Indian Square

The Indian square is a very good kite for beginners, because of its shape and the construction. For the true beginner, you may add a small tail which will slow down the speed of the kite. As you improve in the art of flying, shorten the tail till your expertise allows a tail-less square kite.

The size of the kite will vary according to the builder. The suggested size of this design has been tested so many times that I feel you will be safe to start with it.

The original kite is, of course, a product of India. It is made of coloured paper and is used during the season of kite-flying and fighting.

57 *Indian Square*

Construction

Length   (AB) = 56cm (22^1/$_2$in)

Width   (CD) = 56cm (22^1/$_2$in)

Sides   AC–AD = 39·5cm (15^3/$_4$in)
         CB–DB = 40cm (16in)

Bridle system   AS = 12cm (4^3/$_4$in)
         SI = 32cm (13in)
         BI = 12cm (4^3/$_4$in)
         SH = 32cm (13in)
         IH = 30·5cm (12in)

Bow   CSD = 66cm (26^1/$_2$in)

Fold over the wings   C–D = 7cm (2^3/$_4$in) × 1cm (^{3}/$_8$in)

The bow is made of 3mm (^{1}/$_8$in) bamboo, trimmed to 2mm (^{1}/$_{16}$in) towards the tip of the wings. A 2mm (^{1}/$_{16}$in) fibre will be all right as long as you increase the length of the fold over the wings to cover the bow a little bit more.

The central stick is made with a 3mm (^{1}/$_8$in) bamboo. You may wish to trim it to 2mm (^{1}/$_{16}$in) towards the tail.

If you use a tail to test fly, a soft strip of paper of 2–3m (6–9feet) should give plenty of extra balance. The bridle adjustment will be altered to suit the correct balancing of the kite.

Several types of cover can be used. Always remember that you may wish to fly your fighter kite more than once, so build it to be strong and resistant.

58 *Indian Square construction diagram*

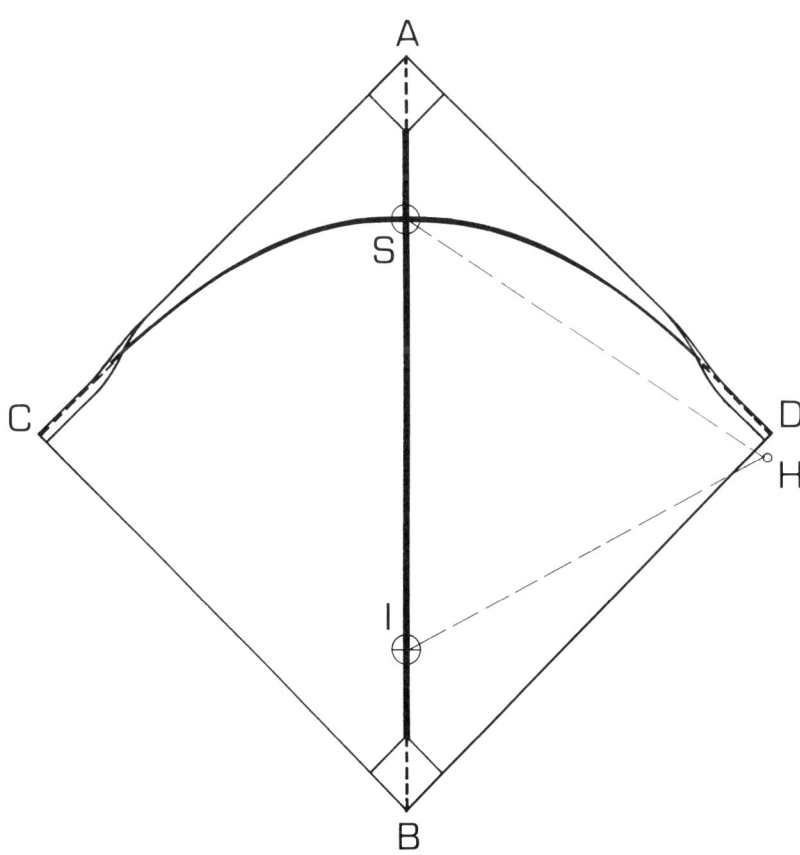

Big Indian Fighter

Two versions are known: the Small Fighter and the Big Fighter. Of the two, I usually choose the smaller one. Maybe my experience leads me to prefer a more rapid fighter with more 'nerve'. The quality of flight for both these kites is remarkable. You will find that flying an Indian-type fighter is similar to driving the best car in the world.

Unfortunately, genuine Indian kites are not so easy to find, and due to the fragility of their construction they are not always in the best of shape. This is why I recommend that you build your own. In order to preserve the fruit of your labours, I suggest you use a robust material.

This fighter will often be your first choice, should the wind permit. If you make it from Mylar or fairly solid paper, do not fly it in strong winds. This kite is fast and very sharp.

As before, your bridle adjustment will have a lot to do with the speed of the flight. A very fine, light Big Indian Kite will fly like a feather in the wind if you play with the hot air pockets and the air currents. I have kept one in the air for several hours while many other kites would not even take off! Try it one day: you will enjoy it and it will give you a superb feeling of control over the elements.

By now you have understood that the bigger the kite, the slower it will travel. Of course this comparison depends on the same type of wind force. The flexibility of the bow and the rigidity of the central stick will also affect the speed of the kite. You should build different types of 'resistance' into the same model in order to have a good kite for several different weather conditions.

59 *Big Indian Fighter*

Construction

Length   AB = 59cm (23$^1/_2$in)

Width   CD = 68cm (27$^1/_4$in)

Sides   AC–AD = 47cm (18$^3/_4$in)
CB–DB = 43cm (17$^1/_4$in)

Tail   EK–FL = 9cm (3$^1/_2$in) (sticks)
GE–GF = 16cm (6$^1/_2$in)
EB–BF = 9·5cm (3$^3/_4$in)
GB = 16cm (6$^1/_2$in)

Bridle system   AS = 10cm (4in)
SH = 23·5cm (9$^1/_2$in)
IH = 26cm (10$^1/_2$in)
IB = 19cm (7$^1/_2$in)

Fold over the wing   C–D = 20cm (8in) × 1cm ($^3/_8$in)

Bow   CSD = 86cm (34$^1/_2$in)

60 *Big Indian Fighter
construction diagram*

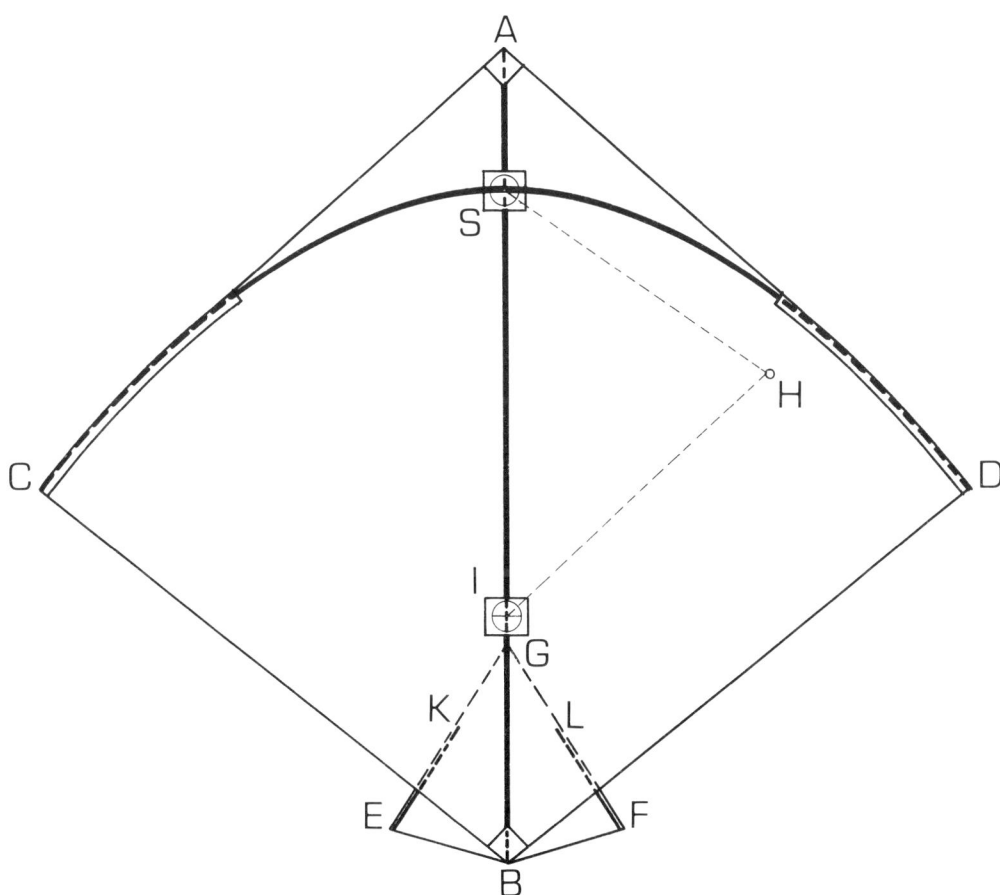

The bow is made with a fibre of 3mm ($^1/_8$in) trimmed to 1·5mm ($^1/_{16}$in) at the tips.
If you use bamboo, try a slightly larger diameter for better resistance of the material. The bow is glued inside the folds. If you wish to take your kite apart for transportation, make small pockets for the bow tips, do not glue!

The central stick is bamboo of 3mm ($^1/_8$in) trimmed to 2mm ($^1/_{10}$in) towards the tail. The two little sticks which are in the tail are made of 2mm ($^1/_{10}$in) bamboo. The spine is glued to the cover. The two tail sticks are kept inside a small fold or glued with extra material.

Always try the final adjustment of the bridle on the first flight so you can get the best result. Once you are satisfied, tie the knot firmly.

Small Indian Fighter

61 Small Indian Fighter

Construction

Length   AB = 45·5cm (18$^1/_4$in)

Width   CD = 53·5cm (21$^1/_2$in)

Sides   AC-AD = 36·5cm (14$^1/_2$in)
            CB-DB = 34cm (13$^1/_2$in)

Tail   EK–FL = 7cm (2$^3/_4$in) (sticks)
         GE–GF = 11cm (4$^1/_2$in)
         EB–BF = 7·5cm (3in)
         GB = 10cm (4in)

Bridle System   AS = 8·5cm (3$^1/_2$in)
                   SH = 22cm (8$^3/_4$in)
                   IH = 20cm (8in)
                   IB = 14cm (5$^1/_2$in)

Fold over the wing   C–D = 14cm (5$^1/_2$in) × 1cm ($^3/_8$in)

Bow   CSD = 65cm (26in)

The bow is made of fibre of 2mm ($^1/_{10}$in) trimmed to 1mm ($^1/_{16}$in) at the tip of the wing. A split bamboo of 3mm ($^1/_8$in) trimmed to 1·5mm ($^1/_{16}$in) can do the same job. Glue the bow tips inside the folds.

The central stick is made of a 2mm ($^1/_{10}$in) bamboo trimmed towards the tail. It should be glued to the cover.

The cover of my model is made with Tyvek. If you use Mylar or light plastic, you will have a much lighter kite.

The two tail sticks are made of 1·5mm ($^1/_{16}$in) bamboo. They are glued to the tail and kept in position by a strip of extra material.

Try to make the Small Indian Fighter as light as possible. The fine flexibility of the bow will give you a very enjoyable kite in light to moderate winds.

I fly my Small Indian Fighter (which is strong and stiff to give high speeds) when the wind is very strong. It is so fast that a good photographer would have to take his photo at 1/1000e. But it would not do very well in a fight, as it is too speedy, and therefore pulls a little too hard on the line, especially in a dive. Still, for good fun, do try it!

62 *Small Indian Fighter construction diagram*

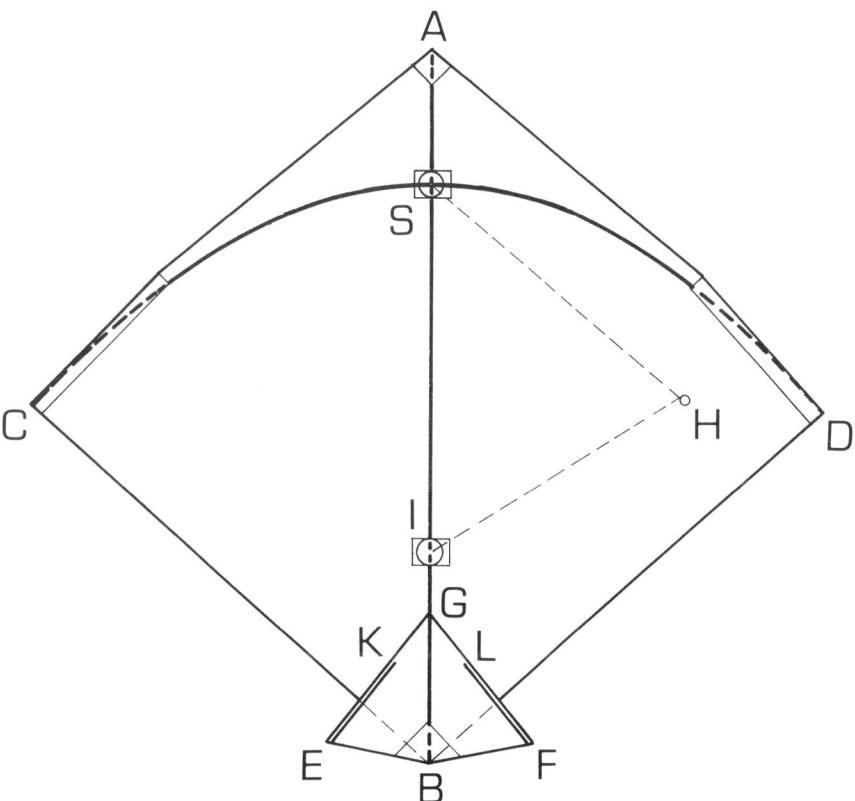

J. M. Favourite (Philippe Gallot)

This is an easy flier for beginners. It can fly in moderate to light winds. My own version of the design is made from see-through Mylar. This allows a very simple decoration with felt-tip pens, with superb results when your kite is in the air as it is transparent.

For the more advanced pilot, a sharper bridle system lets you enjoy the fast turns and precision of the flight.

I am sure that this model, like every other, could be built successfully with tissue paper.

63 *J. M. Favourite*

Construction

Length   AB = 45·5cm (18^1/$_4$in)

Width   CD = 40·5cm (16^1/$_4$in)

Sides   CE–DF = 11cm (4^1/$_2$in)
          EB–FB = 30cm (12in)
          AC–AD = 24cm (9^3/$_4$in)

Bridle System   AS = 6·5cm (2^3/$_4$in)
          BI = 14cm (5^1/$_2$in)
          HS = 19cm (7^1/$_2$in)
          HI = 24cm (9^3/$_4$in)

Bow   CSD = 42·5cm (17in)

Fold over the wing   C-D = 2cm (^{3}/$_4$in) × 1cm (^{3}/$_8$in)

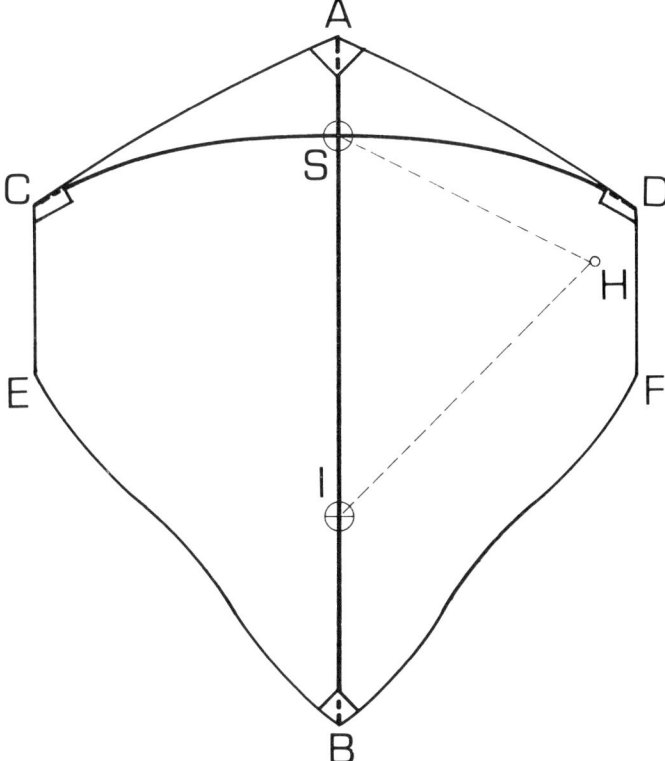

The central stick is made of trimmed and tapered bamboo. I use 3mm × 2mm ($^1/_8$in × $^1/_{10}$in). With tape, secure the stick to the cover. Some special glue could be used.

The bow is either a trimmed and tapered bamboo or a fibre. For the bamboo bow, use a stick of 3mm ($^1/_8$in) trimmed to both tips. If you use a fibre, use a 2mm ($^1/_{10}$in) diameter.

The top and tail parts need to be reinforced with a small triangle of the material used for the construction.

The bow is taped to the cover at the tips only. Put on the bridle, and your kite is ready.

Alert Birdie (Philippe Gallot)

This kite is designed for light to moderate winds. It manoeuvres rather slowly and has a very soft pull on the line. Nevertheless, it is able to take very sharp turns and dives. The name calls for a drawing of a bird with a sharp beak to decorate it.

65 *Alert Birdie*

Construction

Before starting, refer to the chapter on material for the best choice for your requirements.

Length   AB = 53cm (21¹/₄in)

Width   CD = 48cm (19¹/₄in)

Sides   AT–AV = 23cm (9¹/₄in)
TC–VD = 10cm (4in)
CB–BD = 38cm (15¹/₄in)

Bridle System   AS = 17cm (6³/₄in)
BI = 16cm (6¹/₂in)
SH = 15cm (6in)
IH = 19cm (7¹/₂in)

Bow   CSD = 50cm (20in)

Fold over wings   TC-VD = 10cm (4in)

Central stick   Bamboo 3 mm (¹/₈in) thick

Bow   3 mm (¹/₈in) in the centre becoming 1·5mm (¹/₁₆in) at the tip of the wing

Some extra pieces must be glued to reinforce the beak and the tail of the bird. For a novice fighter, the beak must be very strong as it will fall to the ground more often than expected!

As in all fighter kite designs, use a perfect axis of symmetry to cut your shape. The success of your flying depends on this very important rule.

Once your shape is cut, fold the kite in half from beak to tail. Open the shape and glue your vertical stick exactly on the fold.

You will have prepared your stick earlier, using sandpaper to smooth the edges and put the stick in the correct shape.

Next, prepare the bow. Again, use plenty of sandpaper to taper towards the tips of the stick.

Test the strength of the bow. If it is too soft, the kite will fly slowly; if too stiff, the kite will fly very fast and be hard to control. With experience, you should know after a while what kind of bow you need.

Once the bow is in shape, put it on the kite and glue the tips only. The centre of the bow will be attached with the bridle. Your kite is now almost finished.

You need to glue the reinforcement and place the necessary length of string for the bridle. Before cutting your string, refer to the chapter on bridles, where you will find instructions for adjusting and balancing your kite.

Your imagination will allow you to decorate your kite. Remember this one should look like a fierce bird.

If you have used paper to build the kite, test your colours or paint on a spare piece before starting on the actual kite. Remember: the lighter the kite the better it will fly!

Now you are ready for your test flight. Go to an open space, away from trees and electrical wires. Choose a good day and have a go!

66 *Alert Birdie construction diagram*

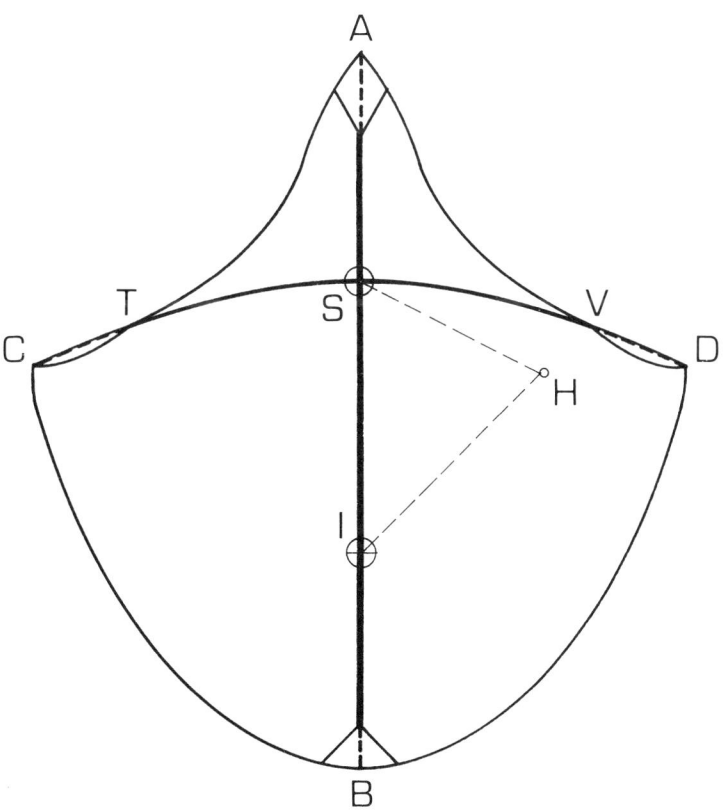

Chilean Fighter (Pedro Fuentes)

Being square-shaped this kite is very similar to the Indian Square. The difference is in the method of flying, as the bridle system is made with two strings fixed on both sides of the bow. This influences the strength and the resistance of the bow. It is a fast kite and could also be classified as a 'strong pulling' one. It will go very well with a good wind. I am sure that a lighter construction will also permit flying in a gentle breeze. For the construction, refer to the chapter on the Indian Square. I would like to thank Dave Ives for the gift of the model he built for me.

67 *Chilean Fighter*

Construction

Length   AB = 52cm (20³/₄in)

Width   CD = 52cm (20³/₄in)

Sides   AC–AD = 36cm (14¹/₂in)
           CB–BD = 36cm (14¹/₂in)

Bow   CSD = 64cm (25¹/₂in)

Bridle System   AS = 9cm (3¹/₂in)
                   AK = 35cm (14in)
                   SI–SJ = 8cm (3¹/₄in)
                   HI–HJ = 43cm (17¹/₄in)
                   HK = 44cm (17¹/₂in)

Fold over the wing   C–D = 12cm (4³/₄in) × 1cm (³/₈in)

The central stick is a trimmed bamboo of 4 × 2mm (¹/₁₆in) and the bow is either a fibre of 3mm (¹/₈in) trimmed at the ends or a similar sized bamboo rod.

The cover can be made with Tyvek, strong paper, plastic or spinnaker sail.

The model I was given is made of nylon and stitched. The advantages of this are tremendous, as it means you can take the kite apart for transportation, and it will have a long life. The disadvantage is that nylon kites have a tendency to stretch if they get wet. Nylon allows you to build strong kites, but they can be a little too heavy to fly in light winds.

Look at Martyn Lawrence's fighter (p.83) to appreciate the work with nylon!

68 *Chilean Fighter construction diagram*

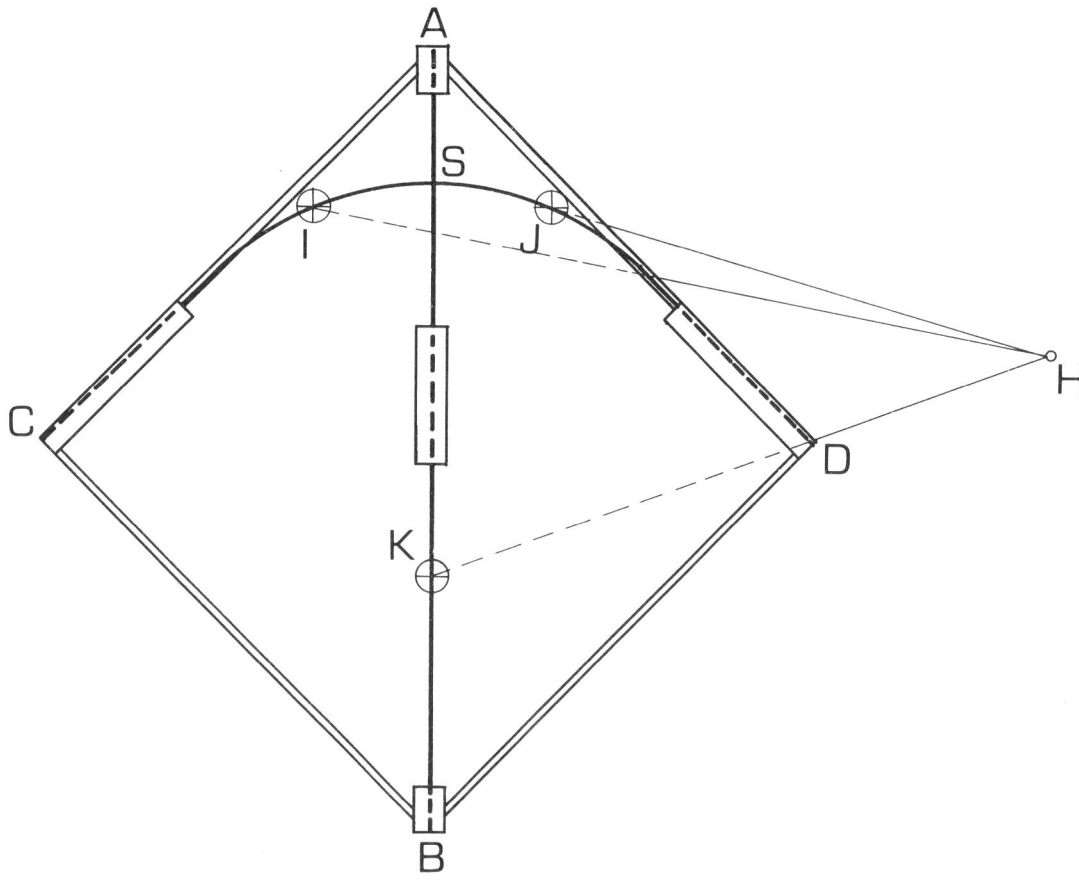

Matt Star Fighter (Philippe Gallot/Matthew de Vogel)

This kite is named in honour of a design made for me by a friend with experience of Indonesian fighters. This small kite is made of very shiny Mylar, so that its glow and shine in the sky attracts the eye. Birds are often puzzled by it and like to come to pay a visit.

This kite is another good one for beginners. Again, a more advanced pilot would adjust the bridle so that it is slightly 'sharper'. It is a good flier in moderate to strong winds.

The Mylar used is the type of wrapping material found in gift shops. Look for patterned Mylar, but even more for its shininess in the sun and the effect such a material can produce with changing orientation to the light. To prevent the Mylar from breaking, I put some reinforcing tape around the edges.

The flying tails are just for decoration. A different type of shiny wrapping material will add new dimension to the kite's appearance.

69 *Matt Star Fighter*

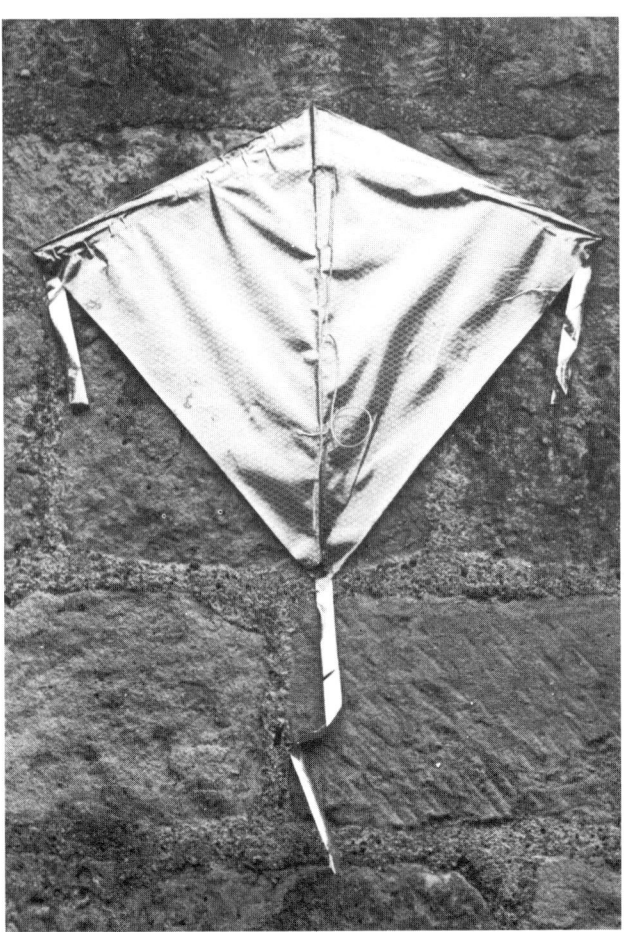

Construction

Length AB = 34cm (13$^{1}/_{2}$in)

Width CD = 40cm (16in)

Sides AC–AD = 23cm (9$^{1}/_{4}$in)
CB–DB = 31·5cm (12$^{1}/_{2}$in)

Alert Birdie

Spear Head

Indian Square

Green Ray

Bridle system   AS = 4·5cm (1³/₄in)
SI = 19·5cm (7³/₄in)
BI = 9·5cm (3³/₄in)
HS = 14cm (5¹/₂in)
HI = 18·5cm (7¹/₂in)

Flying tails   C-D = 13cm (5¹/₄in)
B = 25cm (10in)

Fold over wings   C-D = 10cm (4in) × 2cm (³/₄in)

Bow   CSD = 43cm (17¹/₄in)

The bow is made of bamboo. A well trimmed and fairly soft piece is required for this small kite. Use a 2mm (¹/₁₀in) thickness and trim to 1mm (¹/₁₆in) at the tips. The bow is taped inside the folds.

The central stick is also made of split bamboo. One piece of 2mm (¹/₁₀in) will make a good stick. You may wish to reduce this size to make a much lighter fighter.

The spine is either glued with a special glue or, better still, taped to the cover. Reinforce the front, adjust the bridle and go for your test flight.

70 *Matt Star Fighter construction diagram*

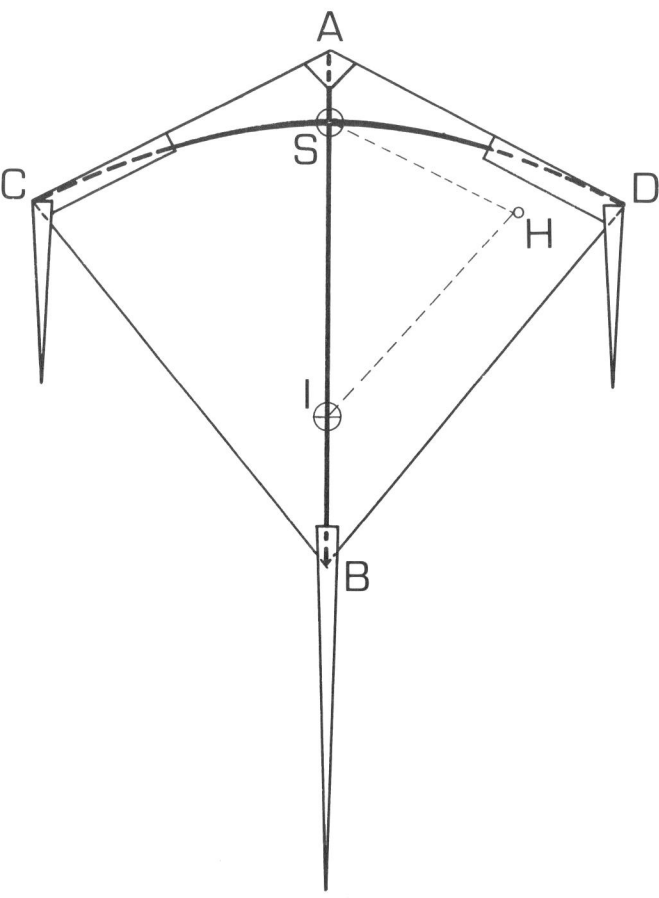

'La Ziza' (Ludovic Petit)

This kite was designed by a friend of mine who is a keen kite fighter and one of my disciples.

I introduced Ludovic to fighters some time ago, and since his first attempt he has been able to draw his own designs and test fly them successfully.

'La Ziza' is a kite for light to moderate winds. It is not suitable for beginners: get some practice in before building this one!

71 *La Ziza*

Construction

Length   AB = 60cm (24in)

Width   CD = 62cm (24³/₄in)

Sides   CB–DB = 34cm (13¹/₂in)
AT–AV = 23·5cm (9¹/₂in)
EF = 12·5cm (5in)
CE–DF = 34cm (13¹/₂in)
EB–FB = 13cm (5¹/₄in)
TV = 35cm (14in)

Bridle system   AS = 9·5cm (3³/₄in)
SH = 34cm (13¹/₂in)
IH = 43cm (17¹/₄in)
BI = 15cm (6in)

Bow   CSD = 73cm (29¹/₄in)
(The bow is glued inside the folds at the tips only)

Tail string   EF = 11cm (4¹/₂in)

Fold over the wings   CT–VD = 18cm (7¹/₄in) × 1cm (³/₈in)

A small string is glued all around this kite to avoid the cover tearing.

The bow is made with a 2 × 3mm (¹/₈in) stick trimmed at its tips. The central stick is made with a 3 × 3mm (¹/₈in) bamboo piece glued to the cover. You can change the material used for the central stick, but if you are not using bamboo for the bow then you must use another very flexible material.

The cover of this kite is made of paper. Several different colours can be mixed to form a patchwork design. Should you wish to made a stronger kite, then you can substitute other types of material (see the chapter on materials).

72 *La Ziza construction diagram*

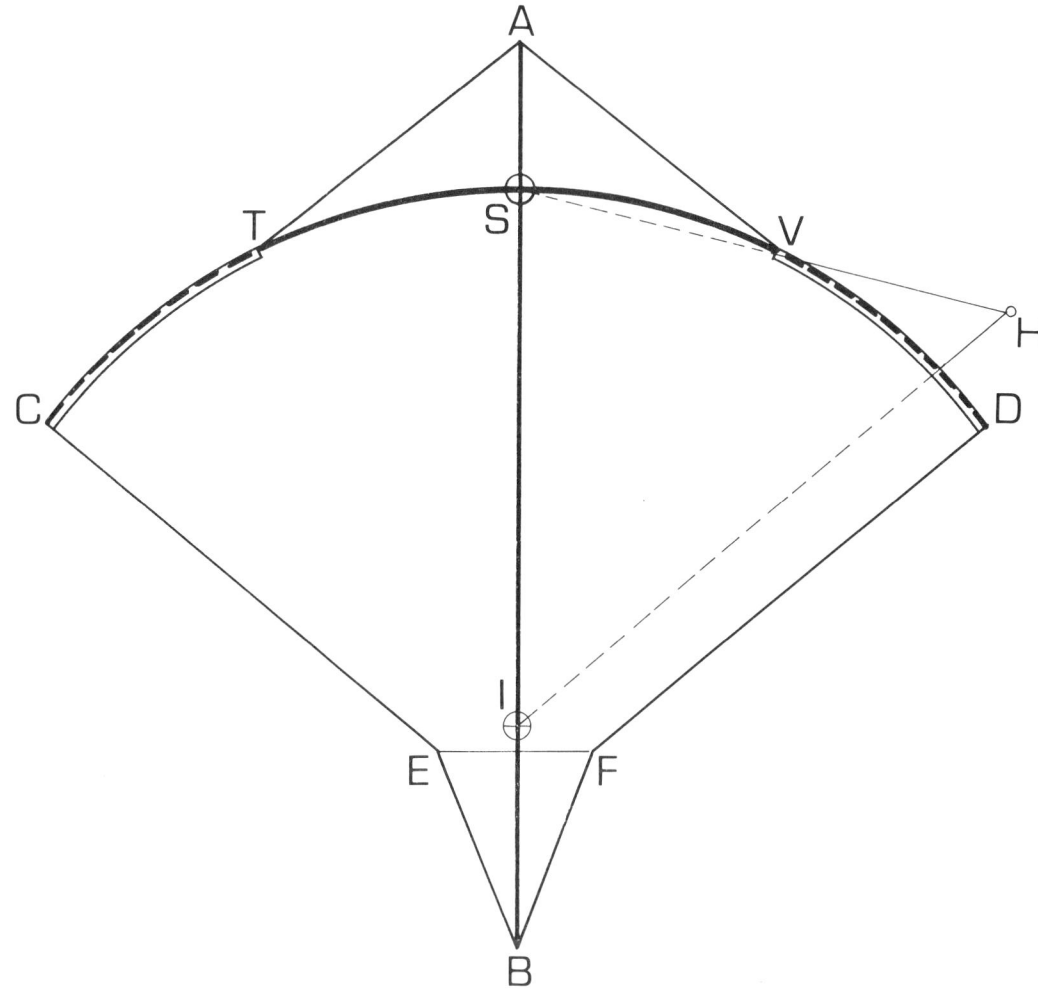

'Le Quetzal' (Ludovic Petit)

Building this fighter requires a little more skill in working with bamboo sticks. It is recommended for fliers with experience and is designed to fly in light to moderate winds. The cover is made of paper.

73 *Le Quetzal*

Construction

Length AB = 60·5cm (24$^1/_4$in)

Width CD = 62·5cm (25in)

Sides AC–AD = 42cm (16$^3/_4$in)
 AT–AV = 23cm (9$^1/_4$in)
 TC–VD = 19cm (7$^1/_2$in)
 TV = 38cm (15$^1/_4$in)
 CB–BD = 44cm (17$^1/_2$in)

Bow CSD = 76cm (30$^1/_2$in)

Bridle system AS = 10·5cm (4$^1/_4$in)
 BI = 15cm (6in)
 SH = 36cm (14$^1/_2$in)
 IH = 49cm (19$^1/_2$in)

Fold over the wings TC–VD = 19cm (7$^1/_2$in)

The bow is a split bamboo of 3mm ($^1/_8$in) trimmed to 2mm ($^1/_{10}$in) at the tips. It will be glued inside the folds.

The central stick is also a split bamboo of 3 × 3mm ($^1/_8$in). The spine is glued to the cover, which will be reinforced at the front and at the tail.

As the kite is built with paper, glue a small string around the cover to prevent rapid destruction. Remember that you should not fly your best paper models under wet weather conditions. You may make several changes to the cover, but remember that a heavy kite will not fly well.

Adjust the bridle and go for your test flight.

74 *Le Quetzal construction diagram*

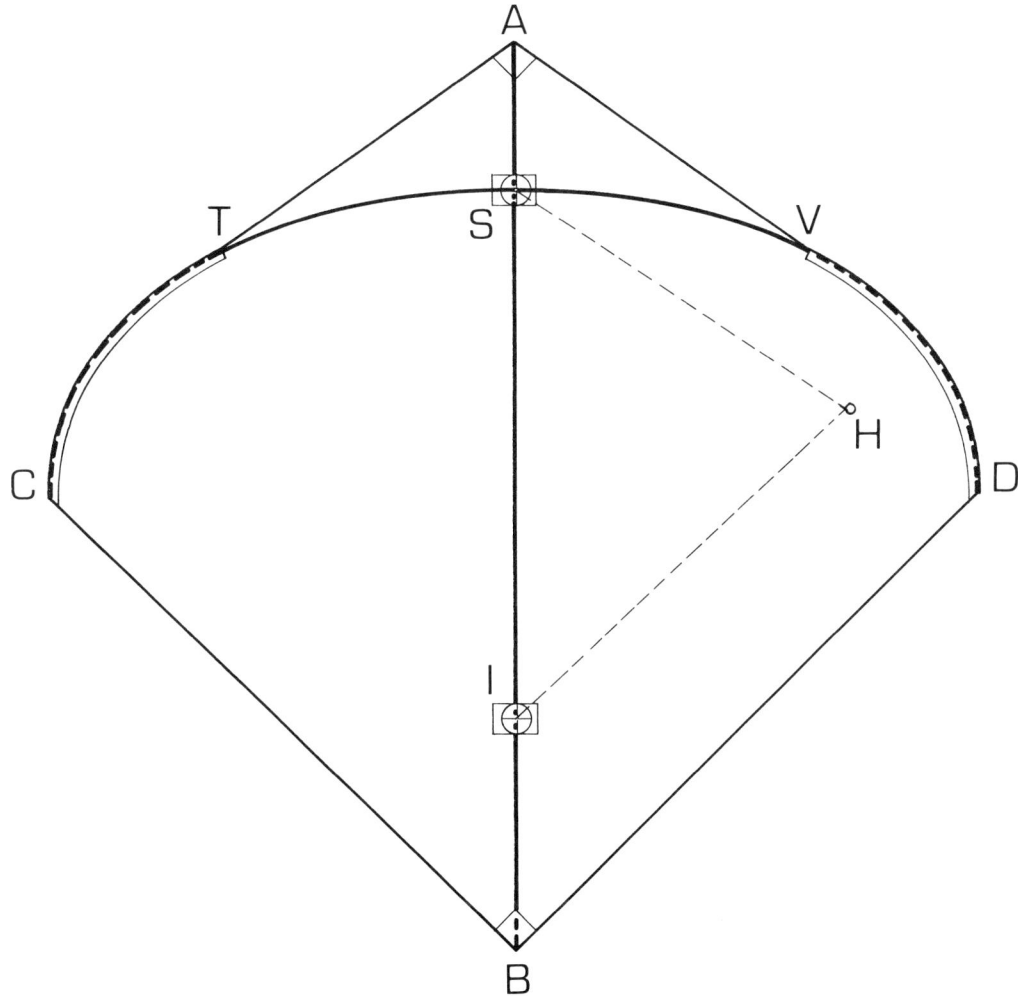

Reims (Philippe Gallot)

The name is better known to the connoisseurs of champagne. In fact this kite was christened as we were driving to Reims for a kite festival. From Paris to Reims is a one and a half hour drive. I took some materials with me and, while my friend was driving, I built this model on the back seat!

This kite is small but not terribly fast, as it has a dragging sail. It is recommended for beginners. If you are more advanced, just readjust the bridle for your comfort.

The cover can be made of fine paper or Tyvek, or even of plastic. The best type is that used for supermarket bags, which is soft and light. Plastic for book covers is all right as long as it does not break when you fold it. It has to be soft! I prefer to use Mylar and Tyvek.

This kite can be built in less than an hour.

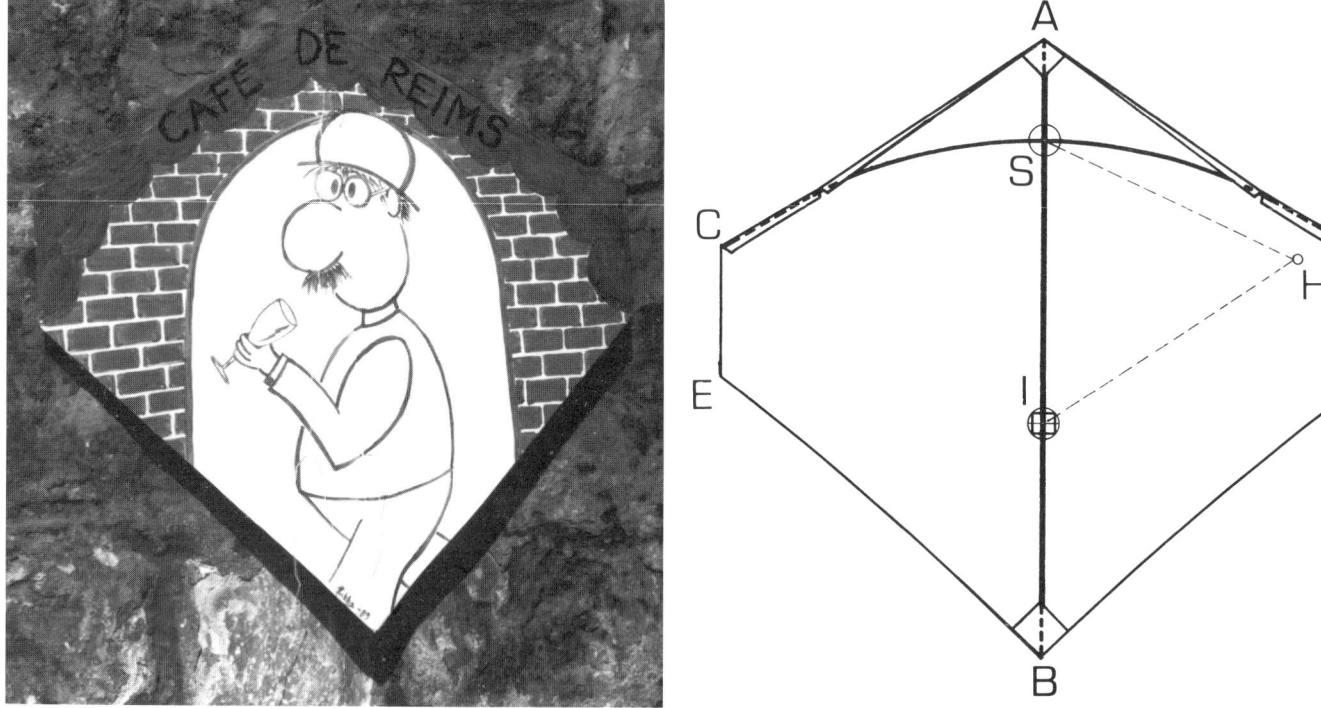

74a *Reims*

75 *Reims construction diagram*

Construction

Length   AB = 41cm (16^1/$_2$in)

Width   CD = 43cm (17^1/$_4$in)

Sides   AC–AD = 25·5cm (10^1/$_4$in)
CE–DF = 8·5cm (3^1/$_2$in)
EB–FB = 28cm (11^1/$_4$in)

Bridle system   AS = 6·5cm (2^1/$_2$in)
SH = 18·5cm (7^1/$_2$in)
IH = 20cm (8in)
IB = 15.5cm (6^1/$_4$in)

Bow   CSD = 46CM (18^1/$_2$in)

Fold over the wing   C–D = 7cm (2^3/$_4$in) × 1cm (^{3}/$_8$in)

The bow is made of bamboo of 2mm (^{1}/$_{10}$in) trimmed to 1mm (^{1}/$_{16}$in) at the tip. If you use fibre, a 2mm (^{1}/$_{10}$in) piece will do, but the kite will be a bit too stiff for light winds. The central stick is made of split bamboo 2mm (^{1}/$_{10}$in) thick.

As this kite is made with Mylar, I use tape to secure the tips of the bow. A special glue is used to keep the central stick on the cover. Reinforce the front and the tail with tape, adjust the bridle and go for your test flight.

McGowan (Philippe Gallot)

This kite is a small fighter, very good for absolute beginners. I called it McGowan in honour of the little girl who produced the drawing for my first kite of this type. She is from Australia, so I call the McGowan my modified Australian fighter. Many children have begun flying fighter kites with this easy model. The more advanced pilot will also enjoy this kite if the bridle and the bow are slightly reshaped and adjusted. The floppy sail makes it a fairly fast kite as well as an easily controllable one.

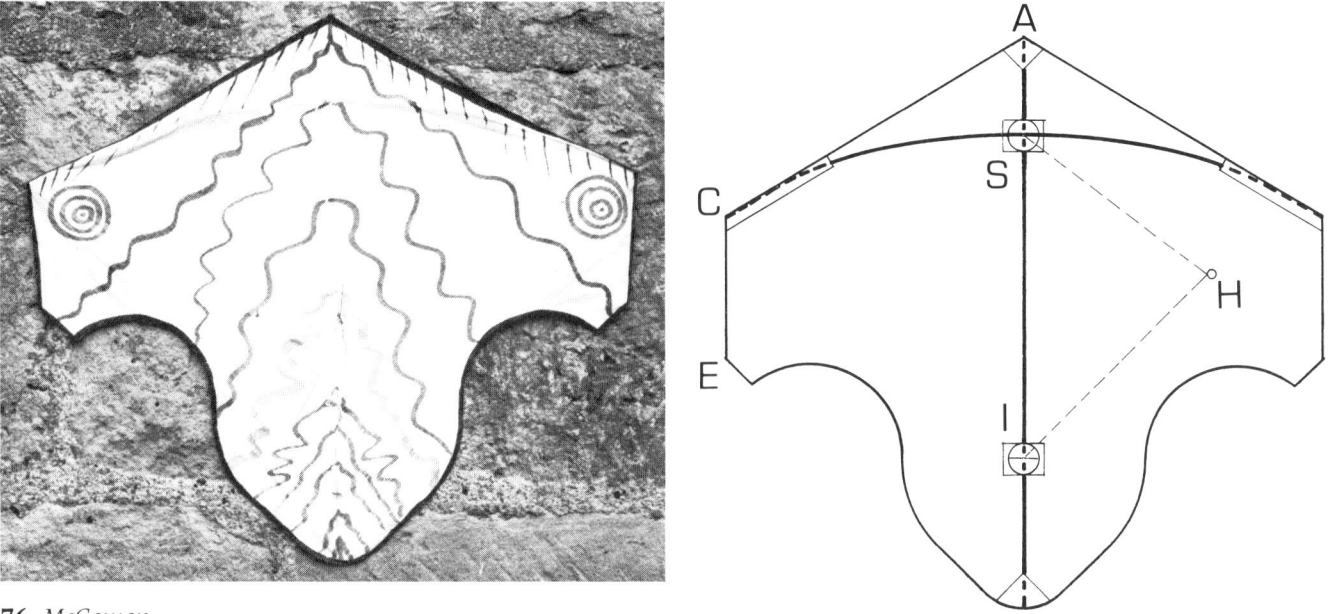

76 *McGowan*

77 *McGowan construction diagram*

Construction

Length   AB = 41cm (16$^1/_2$in)

Width   CD = 44cm (17$^1/_2$in)

Sides   AC–AD = 25·5cm (10$^1/_4$in)
CE–DF = 12·5cm (5in)
AF–AE = 31·5cm (12$^1/_2$in)
EB–FB = 25·5cm (10$^1/_4$in)

Bridle system   AS = 7cm (2$^3/_4$in)
IB = 11cm (4$^1/_2$in)
SH = 17cm (6$^3/_4$in)
HI = 19cm (7$^1/_2$in)

Bow   CSD = 46cm (18$^1/_2$in)

Fold over the wings   C–D = 8·5cm (3$^1/_2$in) × 1cm ($^3/_8$in)

The bow is made with a bamboo of 3mm ($^1/_8$in) trimmed to 2mm ($^1/_{10}$in) to the tips. A fibre of 2mm ($^1/_{10}$in) is ideal. Glue the tips of the bow inside the folds.

The central stick is a bamboo of 3mm ($^1/_8$in) slightly trimmed to the tail. The spine is glued to the cover and reinforced at the front and the tail.

The cover can be made with soft or semi-hard Tyvek. A paper cover is good, but should be reinforced with tape. I have also used Mylar successfully. As the kite is small it can take different types of cover. Adjust your bridle and enjoy your flight.

Green Ray (Philippe Gallot)

This kite is a very slow-moving fighter, because of its large wing-span and surface area. My Green Ray has been designed for light winds. The bow is very soft and the bridle system not as sharp as on a fast fighter kite. This kite would be very good for a novice to intermediate pilot.

78 *Green Ray*

Construction

Length   AB = 62·5cm (25in)

Width   CD = 56·5cm (22$^1/_2$in)

Side   AC–AD = 33·5cm (13$^1/_2$in)
CE–DF = 20cm (8in)
BE–BF = 38·5cm (15$^1/_2$in)
CB–DB = 53cm (21$^1/_4$in)

Bow   CSD = 60cm (24in)

Bridle system   AS = 8cm (3$^1/_4$in)
SI = 30·5cm (12$^1/_4$in)
BI = 24cm (9$^1/_2$in)
HI = 26·5cm (10$^3/_4$in)
SH = 26cm (10$^1/_2$in)

Fold over the wing   C–D = 12cm (4$^3/_4$in) × 1cm ($^3/_8$in)

The bow is made of bamboo 2mm ($^1/_{10}$in) thick trimmed to 1·5mm ($^1/_{16}$in) at the tips of the wings. The central stick is made of 3mm ($^1/_8$in) bamboo, trimmed to 2mm ($^1/_{10}$in) at the tail. You may use other kinds of material for the central stick, but remember that it has to be light. For the bow a 2mm ($^1/_{10}$in) fibre will do a good job.

Glue the tips of the bow inside the folds. The central stick is glued to the cover. Reinforce the front and the tail with extra material.

Once the bridle is adjusted, go for your test flight.

79 *Green Ray construction diagram*

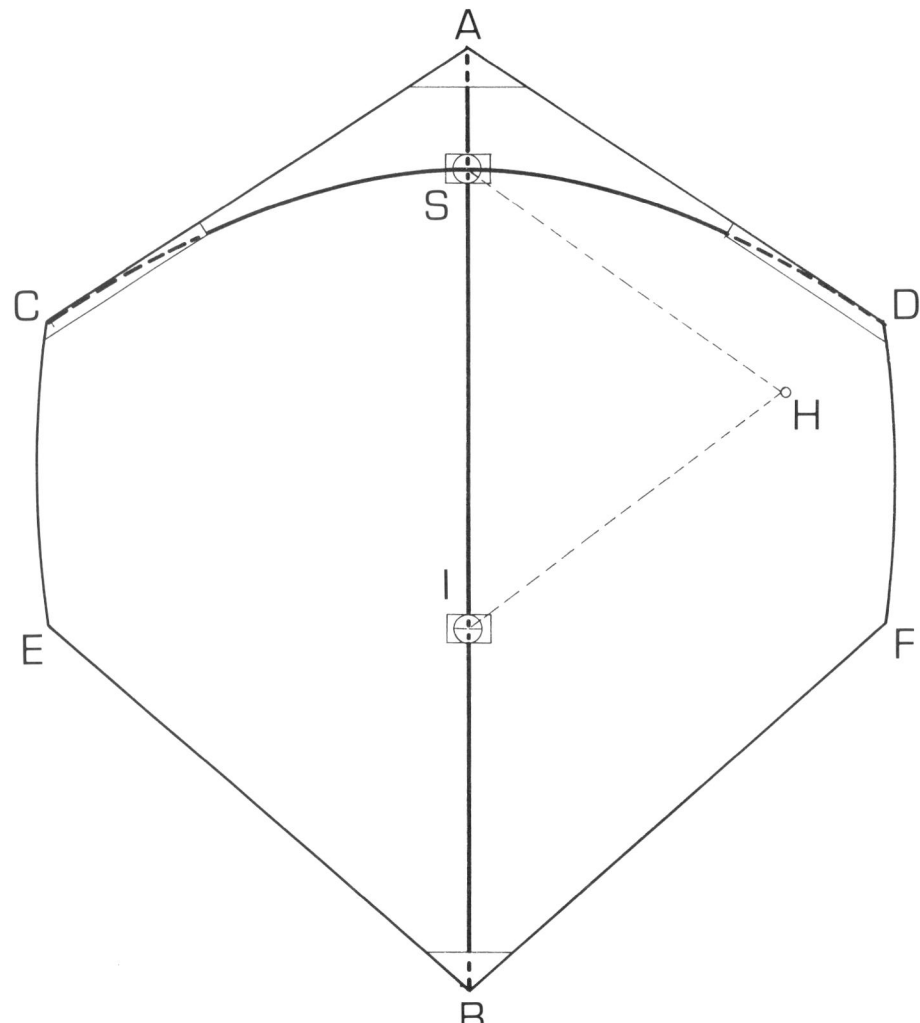

Swift (Philippe Gallot)

The French name for this design is 'Le martinet'. It is decorated with a black and a white tail. A bird's head is drawn on the top making it look like the bird of the same name.

The name was given because of the kite's shape, but also because of its behaviour during flight (like the bird itself). This fighter kite is a very fast one and very sharp to manipulate. The shape and small size give it tremendous speed and quick spins! I would not recommend it for a learner.

You may wish to create a much bigger size, in which case you will need to increase the dimensions by half. You will then have a much more relaxed kite which is easier to fly.

The Swift is designed for moderate to strong winds. It will fly on light windy days but will not respond as well as it should.

80 *Swift*

Construction

Length   AB = 32cm (12³/₄in)
AE-AF = 44cm (17¹/₂in)

Width   CD = 45cm (18in)

Sides   TV = 10cm (4in)
AT–AV = 10cm (4in)
TC–VD = 22cm (8³/₄in)
CE–DF = 27cm (10³/₄in)
EB–FB = 13cm (5¹/₄in)
XB–X'B = 11cm (4³/₈in)

Bridle system   AS = 7cm (2³/₄in)
IB = 7cm (2³/₄in)
SH = 18cm (7¹/₄in)
IH = 19cm (7³/₄in)

Bow   CSD 55cm (22in)

Tail   EF = 14·5cm (5³/₄in)

Fold over wing   C–D = 6cm (2³/₈in) × 1cm (³/₈in)

Before cutting your shape and fixing it to the sticks, do not forget to calculate the need for the extra pieces to fold back. The alternative is to add extra pieces after you have secured the bow in its correct position with clips. This will stop the bow swinging back or sliding while you are in the process of gluing!

The length of the two bridles has been set to 18·5cm (7¹/₂in). The pilot will need to finalize the exact adjustment while testing the kite for its first flight.

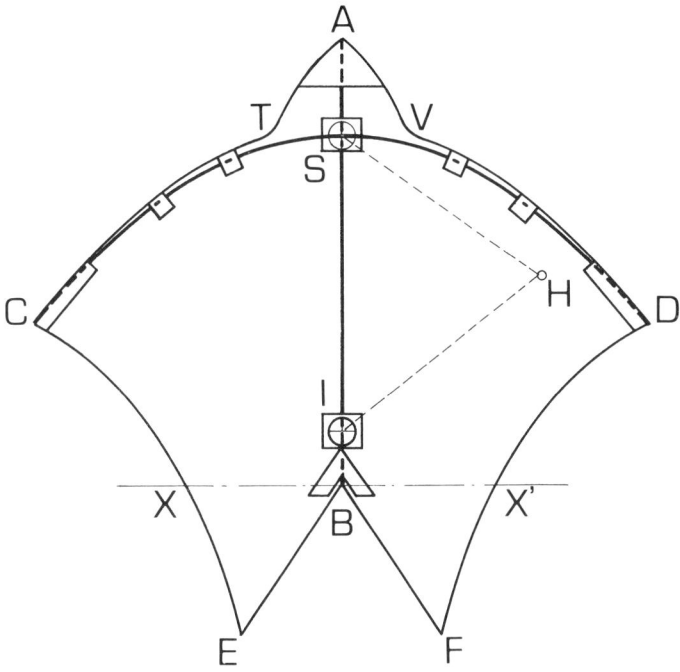

81 Swift construction diagram

Ludo (Philippe Gallot)

This kite is original in shape. It is an excellent fighter but very sharp for a beginner. Its speed and flight remind me of the Small Indian Fighter. The construction must be very light and the bow fairly soft. The Ludo is good for light to moderate winds. I have flown it in strong gusts, but it suffered and was really very difficult to control. Keep this one for good, easy days!

82 Ludo

83 *Ludo construction diagram*

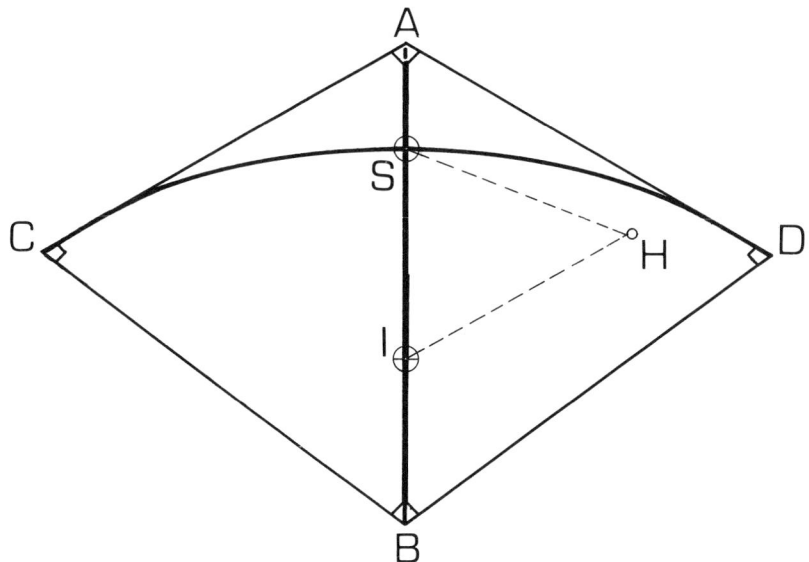

Construction

Length   AB = 32cm (12³/₄in)

Width   CD = 48cm (19¹/₄in)

Sides   AC–AD = 28cm (11¹/₄in)
           CB–BD = 30cm (12in)

Bridle system   AS = 7cm (2³/₄in)
                   SI = 14·5cm (5³/₄in)
                   BI = 11cm (4³/₈in)
                   SH = 15·5cm (6¹/₄in)
                   IH = 17cm (6³/₄in)

Bow   CSD = 51cm (20³/₈in)

Fold over the wings   C–D = 1cm (³/₈in) × 1cm (³/₈in)

The bow is made of 2mm (¹/₁₀in) fibre. A bamboo stick may do, but, to be honest, I have not tried it, as the fibre is exactly the right material and I have chosen it to suit me. The bow is taped to the cover inside the folds.

The central stick is made with a 3mm (¹/₈in) bamboo trimmed to 2mm (¹/₁₀in) towards the tail. Tape the spine to the cover. Reinforce both the front and the tail of the kite. The cover I have used for this kite is Mylar (see-through) so it can be decorated with felt-tip pens and the effect in the sky is superb.

Adjust the bridle and you are ready.

Mini Rokkaku Fighter (Tony Slater)

I call this little Rokkaku kite 'small' because usually this type of kite is known to be rather large: from one to six metres. Some experts fly even bigger Rokkaku. This kite comes from Japan. It is a fighter kite, but is often manipulated by several assistants. The version given here has been made by Tony Slater. You may have your kite ready for a test flight in less than an hour!

The cover is made from a fine plastic bag, and the bows and central stick are built with tapered split bamboo. All around the kite, reinforce the cover with tape. This kite is made to fly in almost every type of wind.

Right
84 *Mini Rokkaku construction diagram*

85 *Mini Rokkaku*

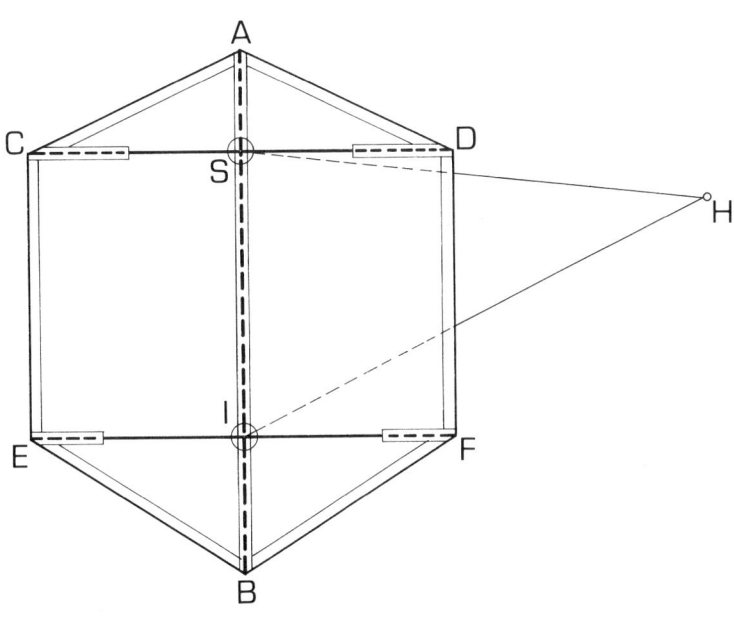

Construction

Length   AB = 46cm (18³/₈in)   *138*   *92*

Width   CD-EF = 38cm (15¹/₄in)   *114*   *76*

Sides   AC–AD = 20cm (8in)   *60*   *40*
       CE–DF = 27cm (10³/₄in)   *81*   *54*
       EB–BF = 22cm (8³/₄in)   *66*

Bows   CD–EF = 38cm (15¹/₄in)   *114*   *76*

The top bow is placed at 9cm (3¹/₂in) from the top. *18*
AS = 9cm (3¹/₂in)
The lower bow is at 12cm (4³/₄in) from the base. *24*
BI = 12cm (4³/₄in)
The two bows are split bamboo 4mm (³/₁₆in) × 2mm(¹/₁₀in) trimmed towards the tips.

The bridle system   SH = 41·5cm (16¹/₂in)   *83*
              IH = 46cm (18³/₈in)   *92*

85a *Mini Korean*

When you have completed the bows and the central stick, start building.

Open your plastic bag and tape it on the table to prevent it moving while you are making your kite. Once you have transferred your measurement to the plastic, tape all around the cover. Then glue (using a glue that does not destroy plastic) the central stick to the cover. Make sure that it is on the axis of symmetry. The glue is to hold the stick in place: using tape, cover both edges of the central stick so that it is well stuck to the cover.

The next step is to fix the two bows. To keep a natural curve in the bows, make a small hole on both sides of the central stick to poke through the cover. Place the bow on the back of the kite (the side which will be facing the wind). Insert the two bows. They should then be glued to the cover and taped over. When making your two bows, be very careful that they are of the same flexibility. Do not make them too thick. We always tend to worry about the bamboo breaking. Believe me, a thin bow will be all right.

Now you just need to attach your string for the bridle. Attach both ends to the junction of the bows and the central sticks. Adjust the length, and you are ready to go for your test flight.

Korean Fighter (Tony Slater)

I do not need to tell you where this kite comes from. This version of the Korean is a very small kite, easy to build and a very good flyer. It does, however need some care to build correctly. You will find that small kites require particular care. Mistakes cannot be hidden when going flying!

The hole in the kite is slightly higher than the exact centre. This is not the case with the normal Korean Fighter. This kite has been modified to suit our requirements by Tony Slater.

As the kite is of very small dimensions, you will need to use a very light material for the cover: e.g. Mylar, polyester, or even very fine paper. All the sticks are made of bamboo. The cover is reinforced all around with tape. The top stick is actually the bow. It should be longer than the width of the kite, in order to be bowed, and kept in shape with a fine piece of string.

Construction

Length   AB = 27·5cm (11in)
        The central stick is 2·5cm ($^1/_{10}$in) × 1mm ($^1/_{16}$in)

Cross sticks   C'F–E'E = 34cm (13$^1/_2$in)
        The sticks are 2·5mm ($^1/_{10}$in) × 1mm ($^1/_{16}$in)

Width   EF = 20·2cm (8$^5/_{16}$in)
        C'E' = 18·6cm (7$^1/_2$in)

Central hole   Diameter = 7·2cm (2$^3/_4$in)
        AO = 13cm (5$^1/_4$in)

Top bow   CD = 21cm (8$^3/_8$in)
        Bamboo 2·5mm ($^1/_{10}$in) x 1mm ($^1/_{16}$in)

Bridle system   SH = 32·2cm (12$^3/_4$in)
        IH = 34·6cm (13$^3/_4$in)
        BI = 6·5cm (2$^1/_2$in)
        AS = 1·8cm ($^3/_4$in)

Once the string is attached to the tips of the bow, you should have 2·8cm (1$^1/_8$in) in the centre from the string to the kite.

Fix the cover on a table or a board. Tape around the design (which will have already been drawn). Cut the centre hole. Glue and tape the top bow. Glue and tape the central stick, also called the spine. Glue and tape the cross sticks. Cut out all around and remove from the board. Make the hole to put the string for the bridle. Adjust the bridle. Bow the top stick. Have a good flight!

86 *Mini Korean construction diagram*

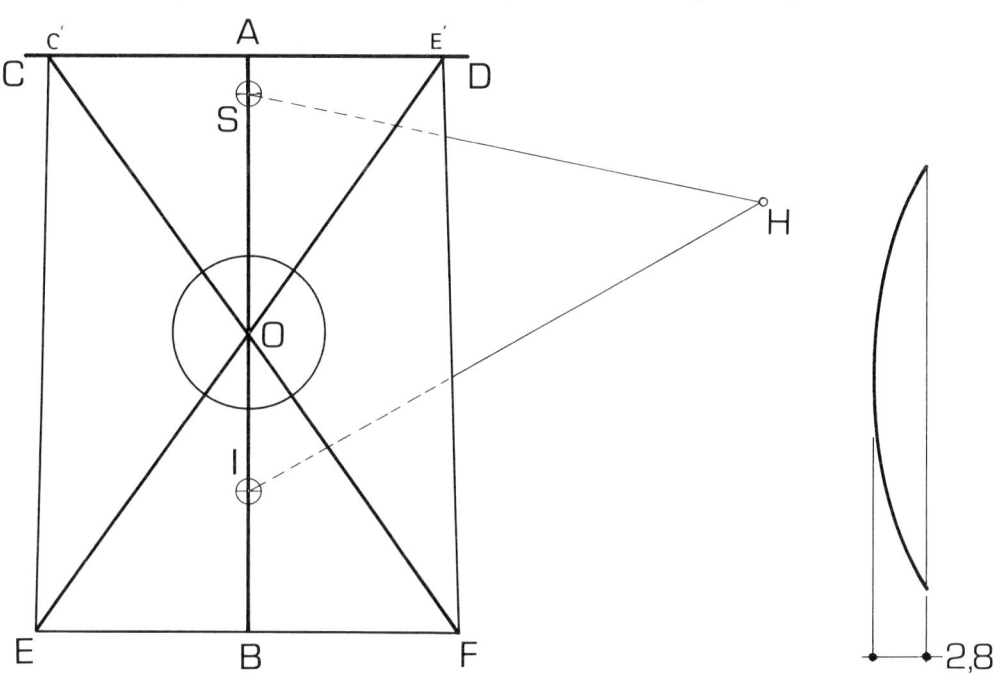

63

Kiwi (Philippe Gallot)

The name Kiwi was given to this design because my first model was decorated with a cut open kiwi fruit. The Kiwi is a large kite. Its construction is simple but requires special attention paid to the tail. The floppy tail makes the kite noisy: when the wind is moderate, it kicks with a beating movement. It also means the flight is not so easy to control. It will be better not to try the Kiwi until after you have a little practice as a pilot.

The Kiwi will fly in light to moderate winds. Turbulent days are out for this kite.

87 *Kiwi*

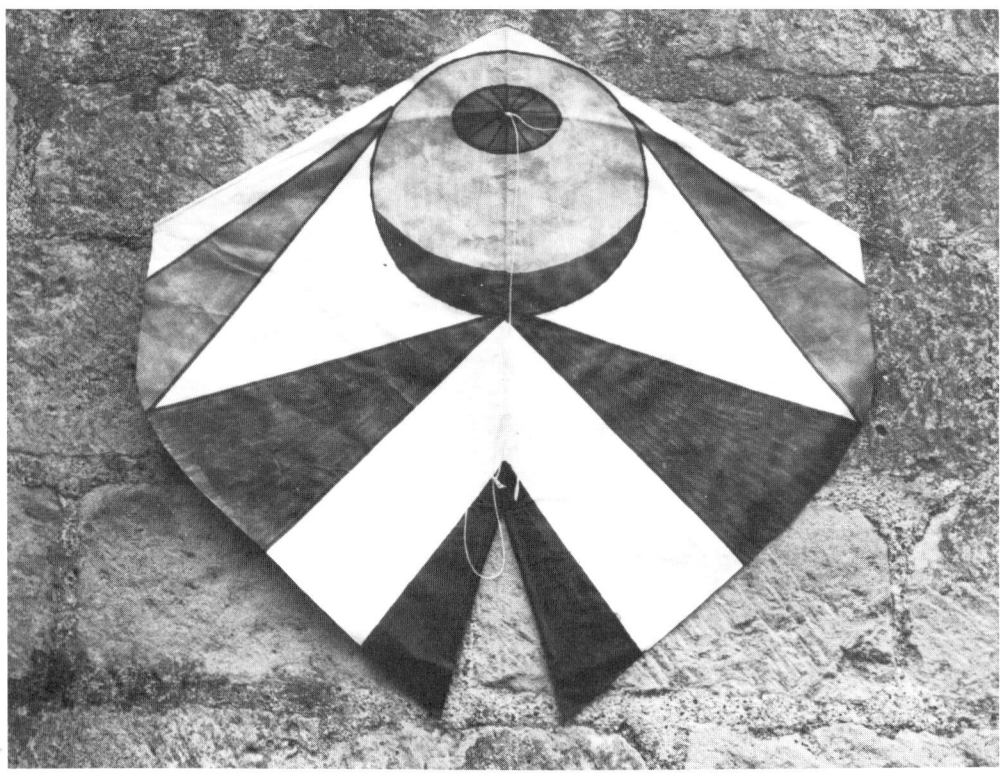

Construction

Length   AB = 56·5cm (22^1/$_2$in)
             AF = 40cm (16in)

Width   CD = 56·5cm (22^1/$_2$in)

Sides   AC–AD = 33cm (13^1/$_4$in)
           CL–DK = 13·5cm (5^3/$_8$in)
           LE–KG = 32cm (12^3/$_4$in)

Tail   FO–FP = 12cm (4^3/$_4$in)
        FE–FG = 17cm (6^3/$_4$in)

Bridle system   AS = 7·5cm (3in)
                SI = 30cm (12in)
                IF = 2cm (^{3}/$_4$in)
                SH = 24·5cm (9^3/$_4$in)
                HI = 28·5cm (11^3/$_8$in)

Large Indian Fighter (Tyvek)

Silver Fighter

Chilean Fighter

Butterfly

Bow   CSD = 60cm (24in)

Fold over wings   C–D = 14cm (5$\frac{1}{2}$in) × 1·5cm ($\frac{1}{2}$in)
FO-FP = 12cm (4$\frac{3}{4}$in) × 2cm ($\frac{3}{4}$in)

The bow is a bamboo or fibre of 2·5mm ($\frac{1}{8}$in) trimmed to 2mm ($\frac{1}{10}$in) at the tips. Glue inside the folds.

The central stick is a split bamboo of 3mm ($\frac{1}{8}$in) trimmed to 2mm ($\frac{1}{10}$in) towards the tail. The spine is glued to the cover and reinforced at the front with extra pieces of material (the same as for the cover). The tail sticks are made of 2mm ($\frac{1}{10}$in) bamboo or fibre. A small fold will house the small stick in which it will be glued.

This kite can be built with paper or Tyvek. If using paper, you may like to make a design with patchwork. With Tyvek you can use colour felt-tip pens or acrylic paints to decorate.

88 *Kiwi construction diagram*

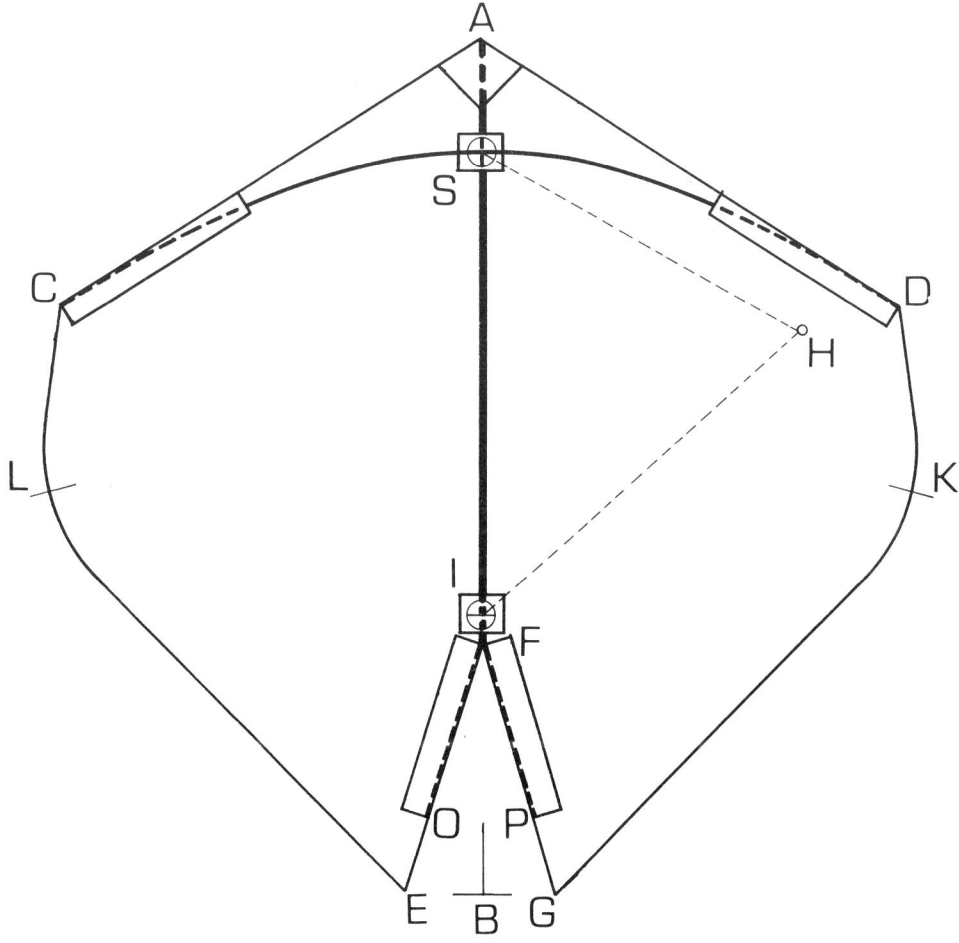

The Red Firebird (Philippe Gallot)

This is a large kite which will fly well in moderate to strong winds. Its name comes from the shape and colours used. In the sky, the kite looks like a bird; sometimes the wind makes it bounce and jump in the draught just like a bird searching for prey. Its size means that it could be classified amongst the more powerful 'pullers'. Careful adjustment of the bridle will correct some of the extra energy that this fighter kite develops.

Paper or plastic may be used to build it. I made my Red Firebird with Tyvek. This allows decoration with a painted design and gives a strong kite, resistant to crashes!

89 *Red Firebird*

Construction

Length   AB = 66cm (26³/₈in)

Width   CD = 63cm (25¹/₄in)

Sides   AT–AV = 10·5cm (4¹/₄in)
TC–VD = 33cm (13¹/₄in)
DF–CE = 40cm (16in)
AC–AD = 43cm (17¹/₄in)

Bridle system   AS = 10cm (4in)
SH = 25·5cm (10¹/₄in)
IB = 27cm (10³/₄in)
IH = 29·5cm (11³/₄in)

Tail   XX' = 14cm (5¹/₂in)
XE-X'F = 9cm (3¹/₂in)x3cm (1¹/₄in)
YY' = 6cm (2¹/₂in)

Bow   CSD = 79cm (31$\frac{1}{2}$in)

Fold over the wings   C–D = 18cm ($7\frac{1}{4}$in) × 1·5cm ($\frac{5}{8}$in)

The bow is made with a split bamboo of 3·5mm ($\frac{1}{8}$in) in the centre trimmed to 2mm ($\frac{1}{10}$in) towards the tip of the wing. If you use a fibre, it needs to be 2·5mm ($\frac{1}{10}$in) or 3mm ($\frac{1}{8}$in) which you have sanded down. Glue the tips inside the folds.

The central stick is a 3mm ($\frac{1}{8}$in) bamboo, glued to the cover.

The 'tail' is floppy and moves about when the kite is flying. You could experiment flying with an additional length of tail. Adjust the bridle and you are ready for your first try.

90 *Red Firebird construction diagram*

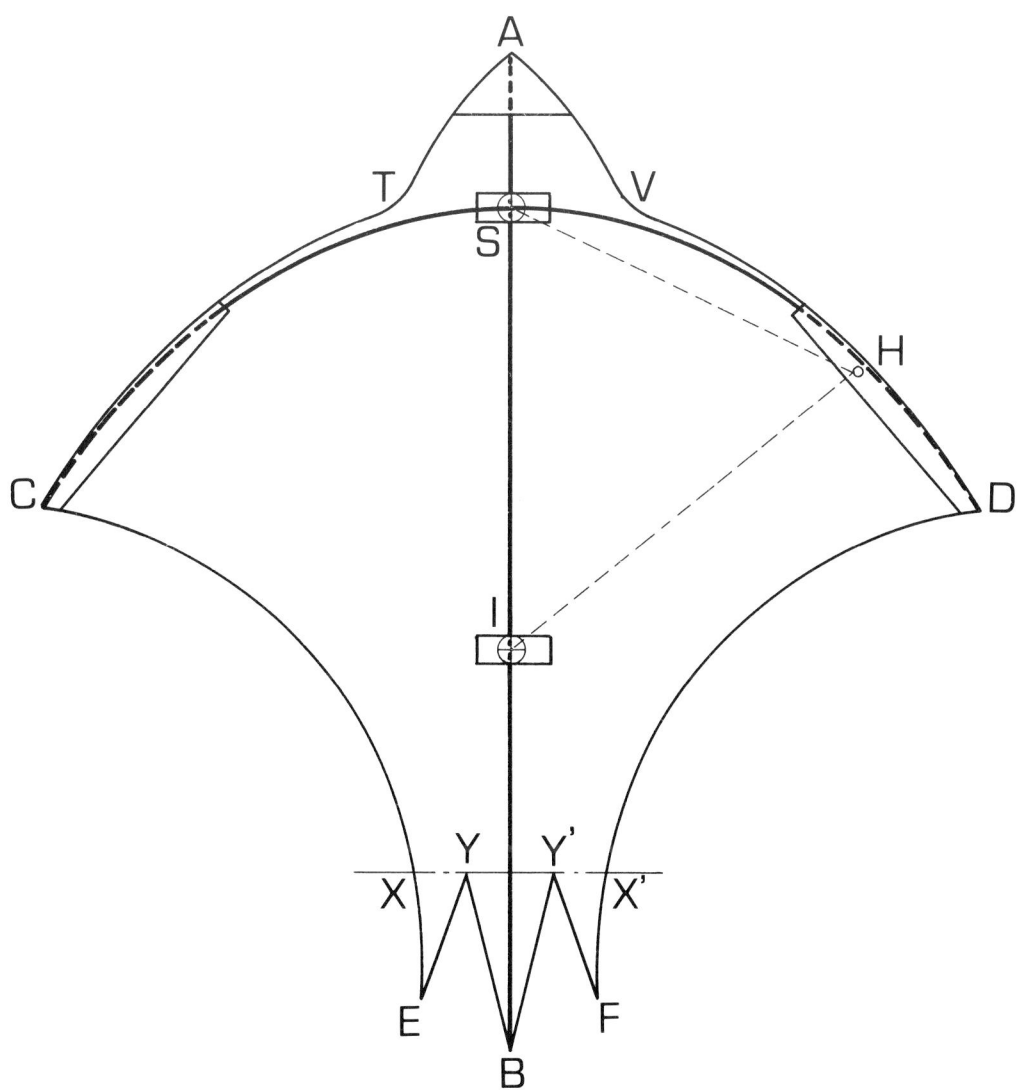

Takeshi Nishibayashi's Rainbow

I have not met Mr Nishibayashi, but he is well-known for his many designs and his kiting enthusiasm. Jim Rowlands mentions Takeshi in his book *Making and Flying Modern Kites*. Takeshi has visited England to give a demonstration of his art, and this is how I came into contact with him. I wish to thank him for his designs for fighter kites which he has allowed to be published here.

The bridle system is very elaborate and allows a very light construction. Takeshi's models are made of plastic and polyester film, using a mixture of bamboo and fibreglass for the rods.

91 *Takeshi Nishibayashi's Rainbow*

Construction

Length   AB = 50·5cm (20$^1/_4$in)

Width   CD = 55cm (22in)

Sides   AC–AD = 40cm (16in)
CE–DF = 35cm (14in)
EB–FB = 3·5cm (1$^1/_2$in)

Bow   CSD = 69cm (27$^1/_2$in)

Bridle system   AS = 10·5cm (4$^1/_4$in)
SI–SJ = 5·5cm (2$^1/_4$in)
AL = 22·5cm (9in)
AK = 40cm (16in)
IH′–JH′ = 11cm (4$^1/_2$in)
LH = 32cm (12$^3/_4$in)
KH = 25cm (10in)
HH′ = 25cm (10in)

Tail sticks FK–EK = 13cm (5$\frac{1}{4}$in)

The sticks do reach as far as the actual letters on the diagram, but are 1cm ($\frac{3}{8}$in) away from the central stick. A 2mm ($\frac{1}{10}$in) fibre or bamboo is adequate.

The central spine is made from two 2mm ($\frac{1}{10}$in) sticks glued side by side and taped over from the top to the tail of the kite. The bow is 2mm ($\frac{1}{10}$in) fibre taped over from one side of the kite to the other. The front and the tail are reinforced with tape.

This kite is fast and needs a good pilot. Keep this model for your more experienced days!

92 *Takeshi Nishibayashi's Rainbow construction diagram*

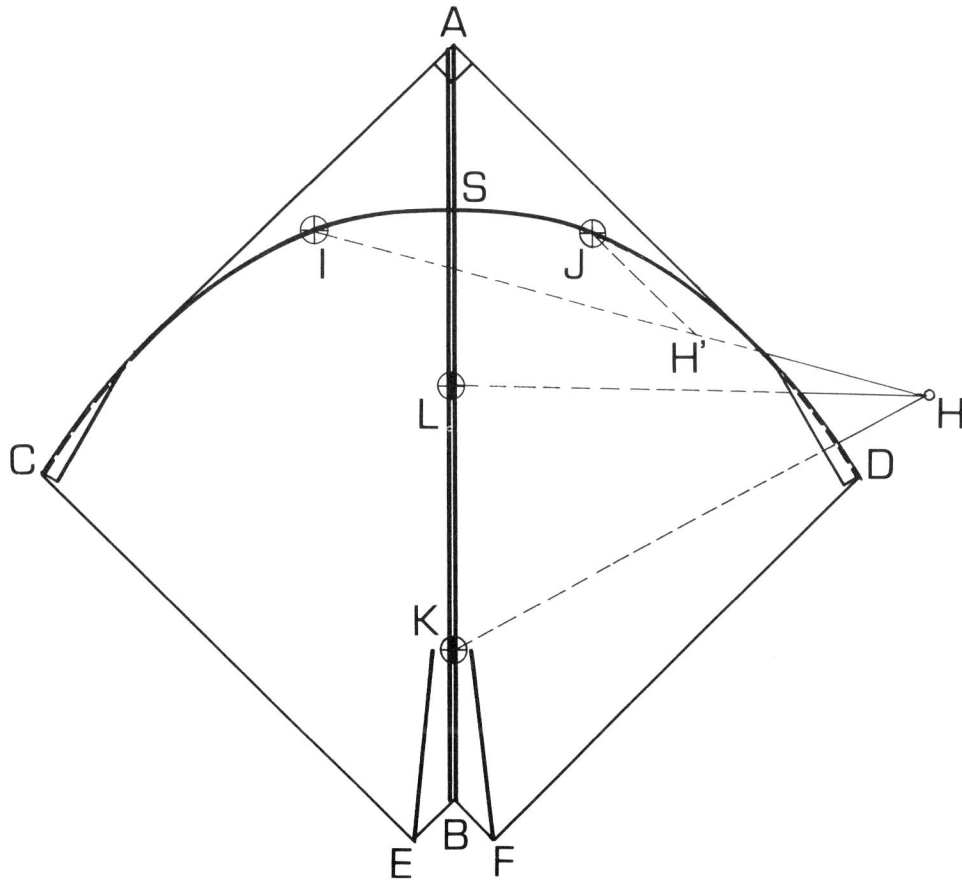

Takeshi Nishibayashi's Large Fighter

93 *Takeshi Nishibayashi's Large Fighter*

Construction

Length   AB = 56cm (22^1/$_2$in)

Width   C'D' = 72cm (28^3/$_4$in)

Sides   AC–AD = 40cm (16in)
AC'–AD' = 50cm (20in)
CC'–DD' = 10cm (4in)
C'L–D'M = 42·5cm (17in)
C'E–D'F = 17cm (6^3/$_4$in)
FB–EB = 27cm (10^3/$_4$in)
CE–DF = 14cm (5^1/$_2$in)

Bridle system   AS = 10.5cm (4^1/$_4$in)
AY = 24cm (9^1/$_2$in)
AI = 43cm (17^1/$_4$in)
SH = 49cm (19^1/$_2$in)
YH = 47cm (18^3/$_4$in)
IH = 52cm (20^3/$_4$in)

Bow   CSD = 69cm (27^1/$_2$in)

The bow is made of 2mm (^{1}/$_{10}$in) fibre. It is taped to the cover from one side of one wing to the end of the other. The extension of the bow is part of the wing front stiffener. The central stick is made of two 2mm (^{1}/$_{10}$in) bamboo sticks glued and taped to the cover.

To stiffen the front of both wings, Takeshi has included a 1mm (^{1}/$_{16}$in) fibre.

The two ends of the wings are very soft and light. The tips of the wings are made with soft, coloured plastic. Takeshi uses a plastic cover for this model. It is a very fine kite to fly.

The bridle system allows a light construction and a very fine flight. The four-leg bridle helps stability and preserves the central stick.

Reinforce the front and tail of the kite with tape.

94 *Takeshi Nishibayashi's Large Fighter construction diagram*

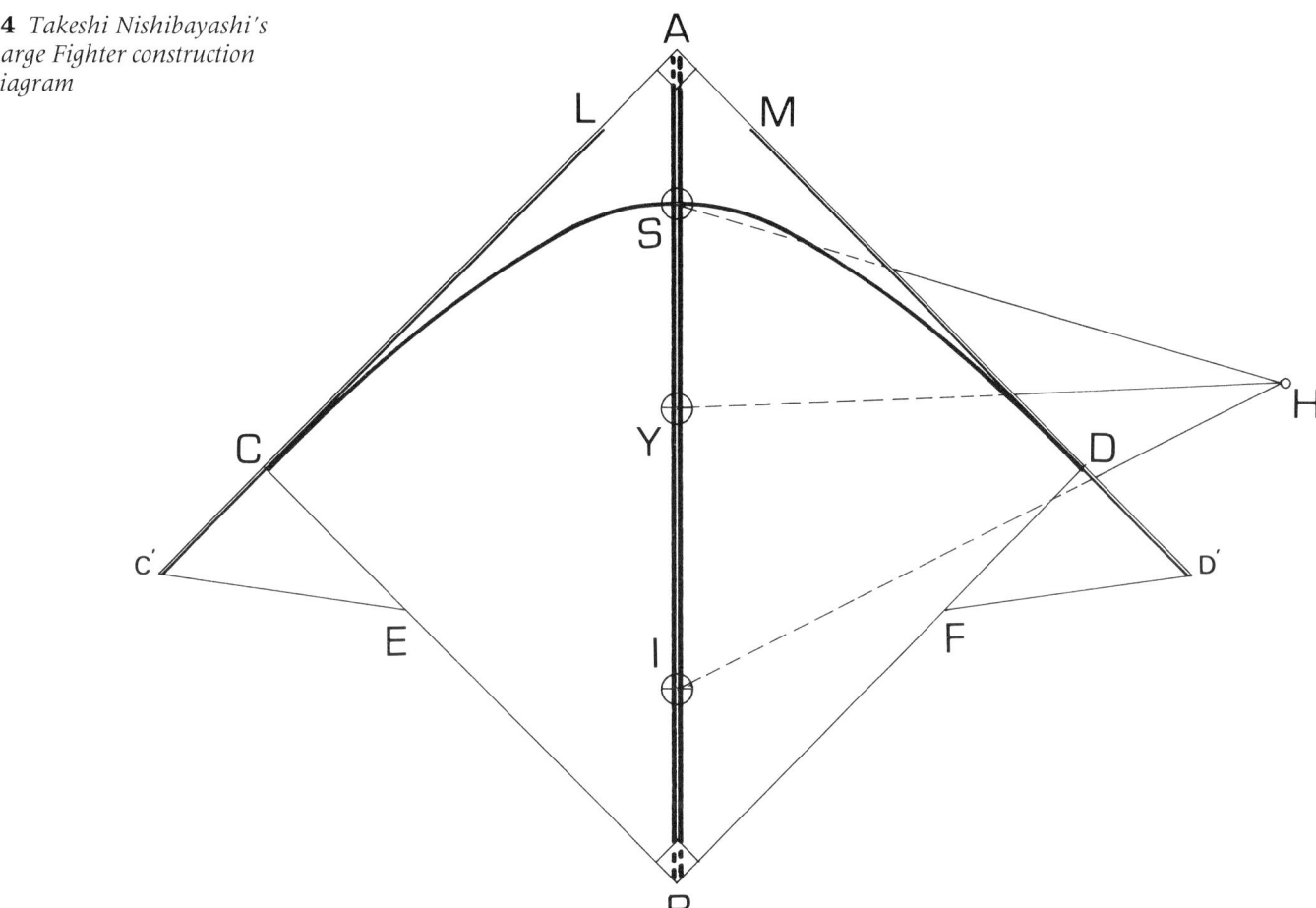

Harpoon (Philippe Gallot)

This is a fairly large kite made for light to moderate winds. The large bow will not take strong winds unless the dimensions are thicker. I use a 2mm ($^1/_{10}$in) fibre. If you want a faster, stronger kite, use a 3mm ($^1/_8$in) fibre. The double tail gives this kite another dimension. If the bridle is set correctly, the kite will be ideal for a beginner. I have used Tyvek for the cover. Plastic and strong paper could also be used.

95 *Harpoon*

Construction

Length   AB = 70cm (28in)

Width   CD = 66cm (26$^1/_2$in)

Sides   AV–AT = 12cm (4$^3/_4$in)
TC–VD = 35cm (14in)
CM–DN = 30cm (12in)
ME–NF = 10cm (4in)
EP–FQ = 12cm (4$^3/_4$in)
PG–QK = 13·5cm (5$^1/_2$in)
GB–BK = 7·5cm (3in)

In order to place the bow in the right position you should measure a diameter:
SO = 32cm (12$^3/_4$in)

Bow   CSD = 90cm (36in)

A fibre 2mm ($^1/_{10}$in) is used. Apply a coat of contact glue to the cover and fold over all the way from T to C and from V to D.
The sticks for the tails are made with a 2mm ($^1/_{10}$in) fibre or split bamboo.

Make sure that the cover can move freely without being trapped by the tail sticks!

Tail sticks   EM–FN = 17cm (6³/₄in)
GP–KQ = 16cm (6³/₈in)

Bridle system   AS = 8cm (3¹/₄in)
SI = 38·5cm (15³/₈in)
IB = 24·5cm (9³/₄in)
SH = 45cm (18in)
IH = 47cm (18³/₄in)
SC–SD = 42·5cm (17in)

I leave a small piece of the central stick protruding at the front of the kite. This gives protection when diving into the ground as well as being useful for games, e.g. when flying to pop balloons. Once the model is finished, decorate it.

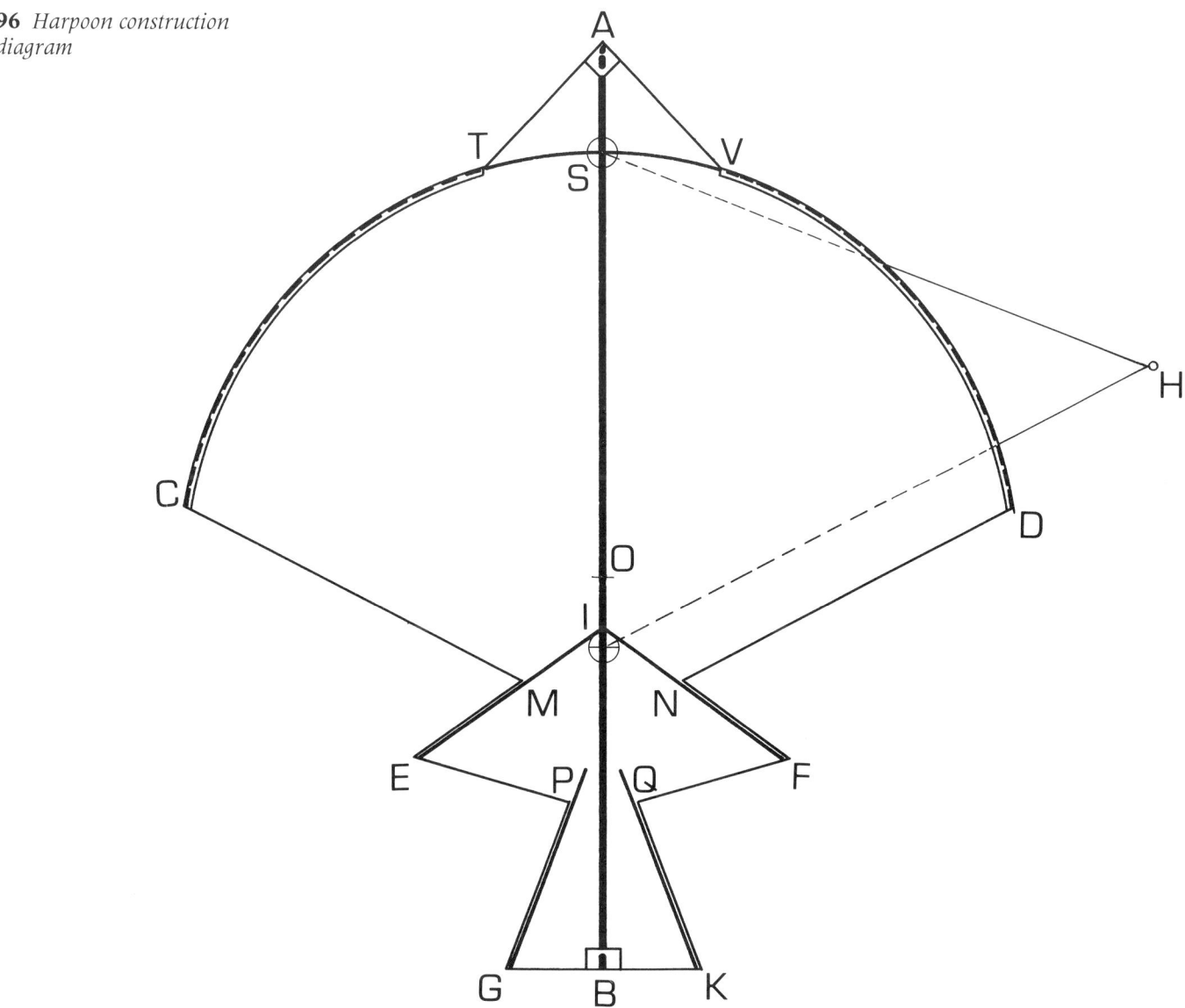

96 *Harpoon construction diagram*

Tony's Silver Fighter (Tony Slater)

I first heard about Tony Slater, a keen fighter kite designer and flyer, when I started the research for this book. I went to meet Tony at his home in England, where I was amazed to see his workshop full of kites of all sorts and shapes. Tony has a superb collection of fighter kites from all over the world. I wish to thank him for the designs which he kindly allowed to be published in my book.

We spent a very good and certainly very memorable day together flying and testing his fighter kites. Tony made a bet with me that he could build a fighter kite in half an hour. I have some experience in building, but frankly, I have never been able to make one that fast. Exactly half an hour later, I was flying Tony's Silver Fighter.

The cover is made with silver polyester (the type used for emergency blankets) and decorated with car spray paint. Tony mixes the bamboo and fibre to create his design. This kite is a very good fighter, and I have entered it in several competitions. In one competition, in Dieppe in September 1988, I flew a kite of this type made of see-through Mylar! It was a superb fight in which I came out the winner. Most of the reward for this was due to the young man who hand-made the cutting-line while on holiday in India; nevertheless this kite itself is very sharp and superb to fly!

97 *Silver Fighter*

Construction

Length AB = 43cm (17$^1/_4$in)

Width CD = 59cm (23$^1/_2$in)

Sides AD–AC = 37cm (14$^3/_4$in)
CB–DB = 36cm (14$^3/_8$in)
EB–GB = 9cm (3$^1/_2$in)
CE–DG = 28cm (11$^1/_4$in)
SG–SE = 30cm (12in)

Tail sticks 2mm ($^1/_{10}$in) square:
FE–FG = 9cm (3$^1/_2$in)

Bow CSD = 63cm (25$^1/_4$in)

Bridle systems SI = 22cm (8$^3/_4$in)
SB = 39cm (15$^1/_2$in)
AS = 10cm (4in)
SH = 30cm (12in)
IH = 32cm (12$^3/_4$in)
AF = 34·5cm (13$^3/_4$in)

Reinforce the tips of the wings over 9cm (3$^1/_2$in).

The front of the kite should be strong. Put on extra tape to prevent breaking in the event of a fast collision with the ground! The entire kite is reinforced with clear tape to strengthen the sides. If you wish to use a different type of material, first try its resistance to breaking so you know where you will need extra tape!

The bow is made with a 2mm ($^1/_{10}$in) fibre. The central stick is of 4mm ($^3/_{16}$in) × 2mm ($^1/_{10}$in) bamboo. The tail sticks are made of 2mm ($^1/_{10}$in) bamboo.

You may wish to adjust the bridle, so always leave an extra piece of string hanging free after you have made your knot. The sticks are glued and taped to the cover.

98 *Silver Fighter construction diagram*

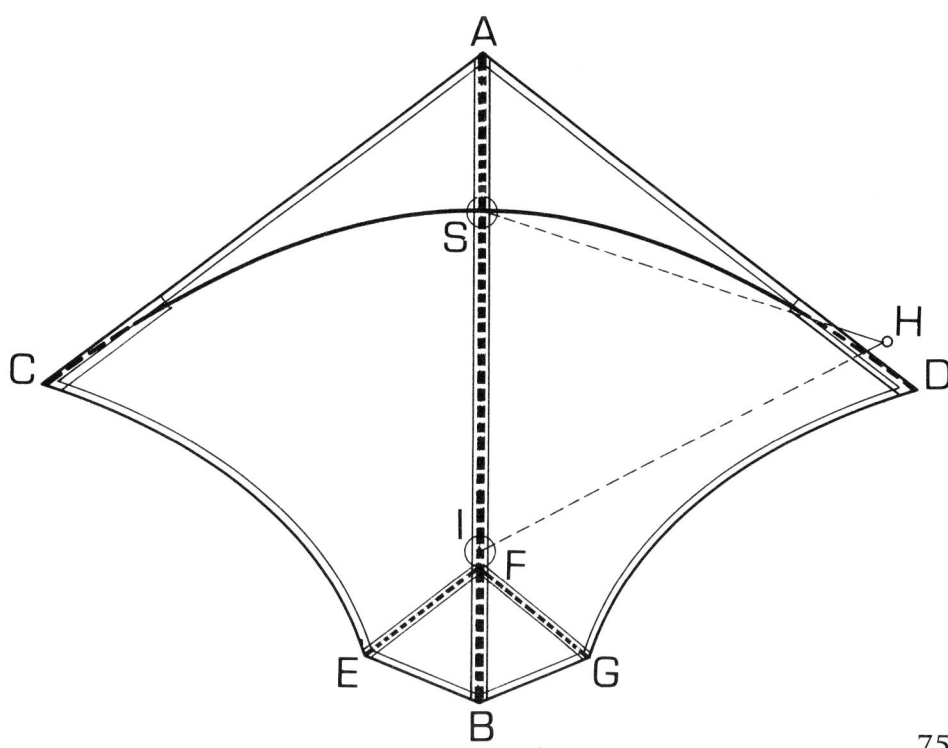

Tony's Butterfly (Tony Slater)

This kite is an excellent fighter. It takes more time and preparation to build than the Silver Fighter, but flies well and is very suitable for a beginner. This kite is fairly small and has a gentle pull on the string. The decoration is obvious: make the kite look like a real butterfly. Tony uses spray paint for this.

99 *Butterfly*

Construction

Length   AB = 36·5cm (14$^1/_2$in)

Width   CD = 63cm (25$^1/_4$in)

Bow   CSD = 69cm (27$^1/_2$in)
The bow is taped over 12cm (4$^3/_4$in) from the tip of the wing. The bow is a 2mm ($^1/_{10}$in) fibre.

Sides   AC–AD = 37cm (14$^3/_4$in)
CK–DK′ = 21cm (8$^3/_8$in)
KL–K′L′ = 10cm (4in)
SK–SK′ = 27cm (10$^3/_4$in)
SL–SL′ = 33cm (13$^1/_4$in)
GG′ = 20cm (8in)
BG–BG′ = 16cm (6$^3/_8$in)
KK′ = 28cm (11$^1/_4$in)
LL′ = 20cm (8in)

Tail   LG-L′G′ = 10cm (4in)
BF–BF′ = 4cm (1$^1/_2$in)
The tail pieces are 2cm ($^3/_4$in) wide
The tail sticks, G–G′ = 23cm (9$^1/_4$in)
The antennae are made with rattan cane. SY–SY′ = 15cm (6in)

Bridle system   AS = 7·5cm (3in)
SI = 21·5cm (8½in)
IB = 7·5cm (3in)
SH = 30cm (12in)
HI = 30cm (12in)

The original kite was made with white polyester film, but other types of material could also be used.

The central stick is made of a trimmed bamboo, 4mm (³/₁₆in) × 2mm (¹/₁₀in).

The kite is reinforced all around with tape. The 3mm (¹/₈in) tail rattan sticks are stuck with tape, as are the antennae. In order to make a strong 'nose', the front of the kite is also reinforced.

100 *Butterfly construction diagram*

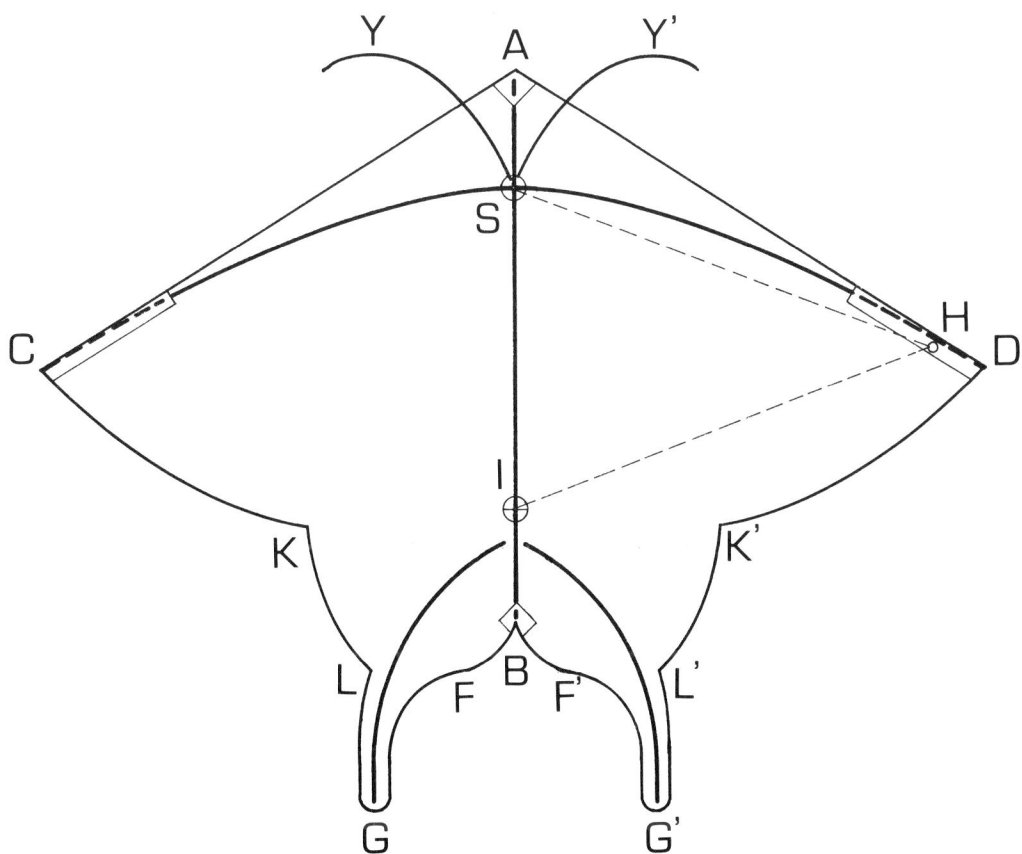

Spear Head (Philippe Gallot)

The original name for this large kite is 'Fer de lance'. It is fast and has a fairly strong pull. If you fly a strong pulling kite in combat, you may not always find it easy to escape. You will be vulnerable if you fly heavy kites. Here again, the adjustment of the bridle may have a lot to do with the strength of the kite.

However, this type of kite does not handle fast. As with most fighters, the bigger the size, the slower it moves. This one could be a good one for training.

101 *Spear Head*

Construction

Length   AB = 63cm (25$^1/_4$in)

Width   CD = 70cm (28in)

Sides   AC–AD = 50cm (20in)

Tail   E–F = 22cm (8$^3/_4$in)
    AF–AE = 60cm (24in)
    CE–DF = 34cm (13$^1/_2$in)

Tail sticks   EG-FG = 16cm (6$^3/_8$in)

Bridle system   BG = 16cm (6$^3/_8$in)
    AS = 13cm (5$^1/_4$in)
    BI = 24·5cm (9$^3/_4$in)
    SI = 25cm (10in)
    SH = 22cm (8$^3/_4$in)
    IH = 25·5cm (10$^1/_4$in)

Bow   CSD = 86cm (34$^3/_8$in)

Fold over the wings   C = 14cm (5$^1/_2$in) × 2cm ($^3/_4$in)
    D = 14cm (5$^1/_2$in) × 2cm ($^3/_4$in)

The kite can be built with Tyvek or plastic. If you use paper, a string should be included all around the kite to prevent it tearing. For this kite I recommend a strong material, as it is usually better to build a kite to last more than a few flights!

The bow is made of 3mm ($^1/_8$in) fibre trimmed to 2mm ($^1/_{10}$in) at the tips of the wings, while the central stick is made of 3mm ($^1/_8$in) bamboo trimmed to 2mm ($^1/_{10}$in) towards the tail.

The two sticks for the tail are made of either a 2mm ($^1/_{10}$in) bamboo or a piece of fibre of the same size.

Once again, adjust the bridle to suit your abilities.

102 *Spear Head construction diagram*

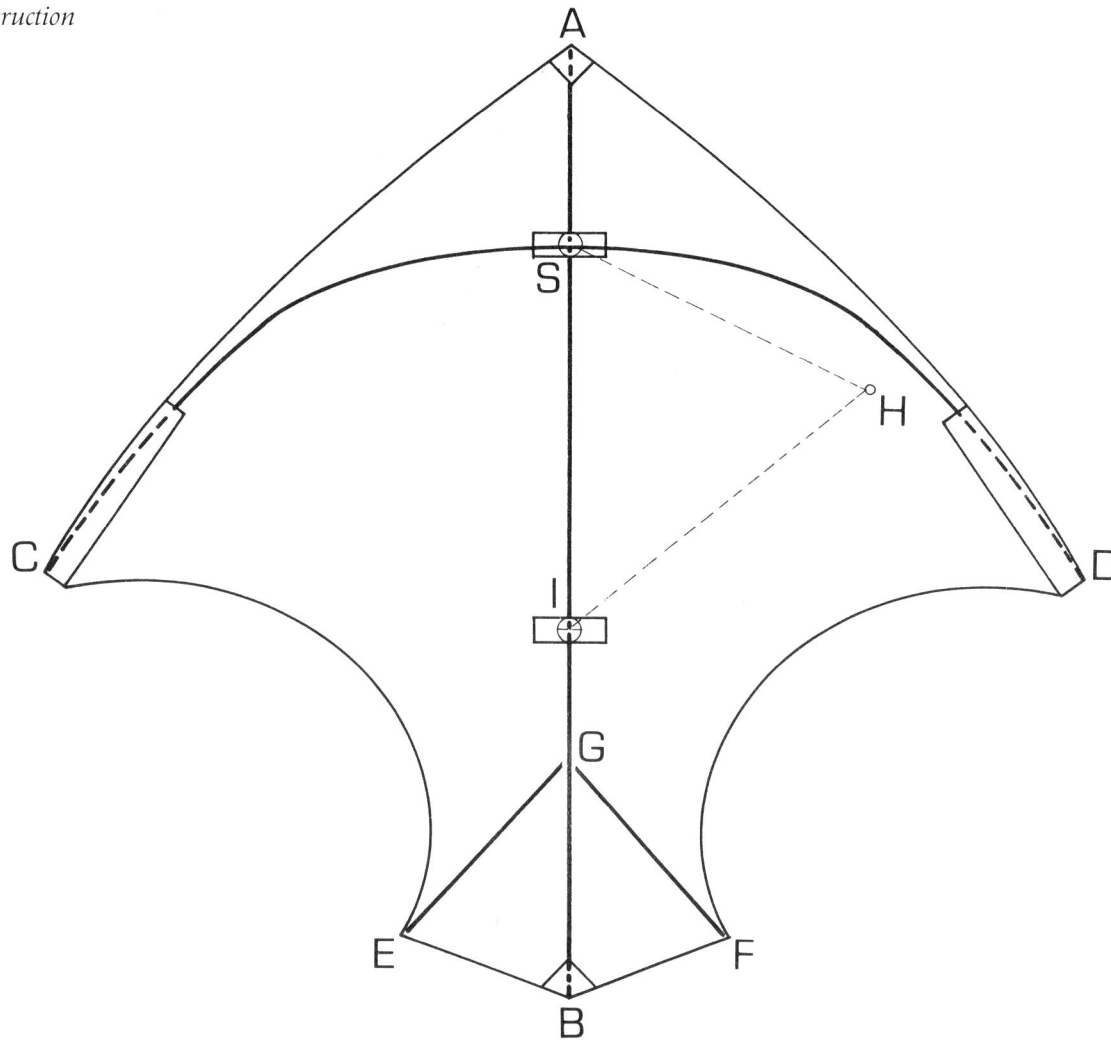

Sang-Froid (Philippe Gallot)

This kite is called 'Sang-Froid'because it is red and a 'sneaky' flier. It is rather large and gives a fairly strong pull on the line.

I think it would be a vulnerable kite to fly in a championship. I have designed this model in order to give myself practice in flying stronger kites. If the bridle system is well adjusted, this kite will be ideal for a learner pilot. Because it is larger than most of the usual fighter kites, it flies 'slowly' giving you more time to control it.

I use nylon spinnaker sail to make the cover. Paper and plastic will also do.

Remember, if you are a starter in fighter building, flying will take a few tries before you get it right. Therefore build with a robust material to preserve your efforts.

103 *Sang-Froid*

Construction

Length AB = 67cm (26^3/$_4$in)

Width CD = 72cm (28^3/$_4$in)

Sides AT–AV = 23cm (9^1/$_4$in)
TC–VD = 24cm (9^1/$_2$in)
CE–DF = 12cm (4^3/$_4$in)
EB–FB = 44cm (17^1/$_2$in)

Bridle system AS = 14cm (5^1/$_2$in)
IB = 22cm (8^3/$_4$in)
SH = 26cm (10^3/$_8$in)
IH = 32cm (12^3/$_4$in)

Bow CSD = 80cm (32in)

Moustache for the wings and tail (for decoration and visual effects in the air – these
do not affect the actual stability of the kite)
EK–FL = 2·5cm (1in) × 18cm (7^1/$_4$in)
BM–BN = 2·5cm (1in) × 23cm (9^1/$_4$in)

Fold over the wing CT = DV = 21cm (8^3/$_8$in)

The central stick is made of split bamboo of 4mm (^{3}/$_{16}$in) × 2·5mm (^{1}/$_{10}$in),
trimmed and tapered towards the tail. The stick is glued to the cover and taped
over for safety.

The bow is made with a fibre of 3mm (^{1}/$_8$in) which I have refined towards the
tips to 2mm (^{1}/$_{10}$in). It is stuck with contact glue to the cover and trapped inside
the folds.

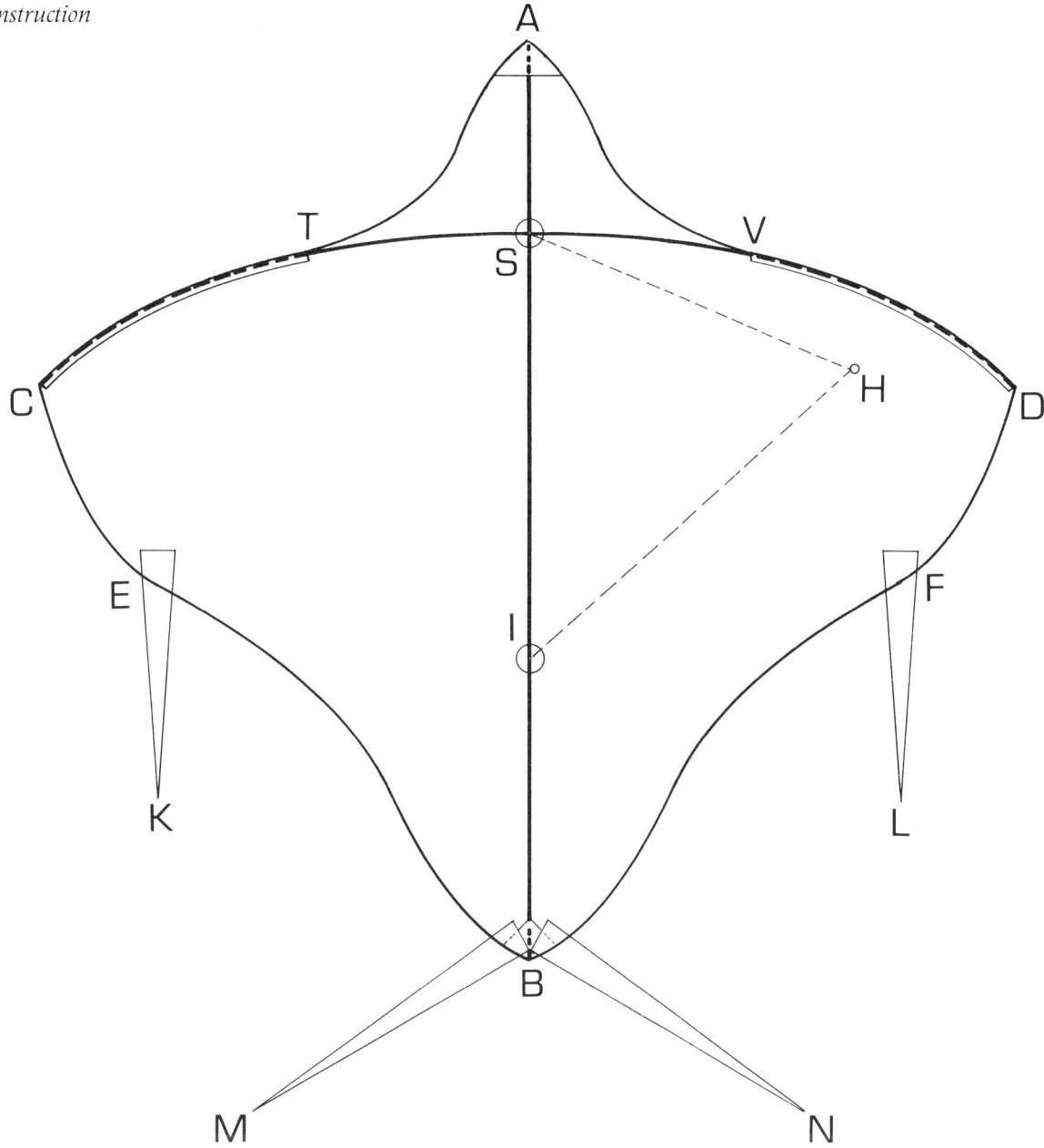

Ti Tomah (Philippe Gallot)

The Ti Tomah is a very small fighter kite, and belongs in the section on mini kites. It is designed to fly in very light winds. Funnily enough, I have tried Ti Tomah in strong winds and, in spite of its small size and very light structure, it went extremely well! Because the kite is small, it does not pull on the line. The pilot therefore has to manipulate the line as if it were lead crystal!

Construction

Length   AB = 19·5cm (7³/₄in)

Width   CD = 38cm (15¹/₄in)

Sides   AD–AC = 22cm (8³/₄in)
CE–DF = 18cm (7¹/₄in)
EB–BF = 4·5cm (1³/₄in)

Tail   EF = 7·5cm (3in)
EK–FL = 5·5cm (2¹/₄in)
KL = 4·5cm (1³/₄in)

Bow   CSD = 41cm (16³/₈in)
Taped over the tips of the bow = 10cm (4in)

Bridle system   AS = 4cm (1¹/₂in)
SI = 11·5cm (4¹/₂in)
SH = 22cm (8³/₄in)
IH = 21·5cm (8¹/₂in)

The cover is made of very fine plastic. The bow is a bamboo of 1·5mm (¹/₁₆in) and the central stick is a bamboo of 2mm (¹/₁₀in). The cover is taped all round. Both the bow and the spine are kept in place with tape. The two sticks for the tail are either fibre or bamboo of 1mm (¹/₃₂in). The bridle thread is very fine.

106 *Ti Tomah construction diagram*

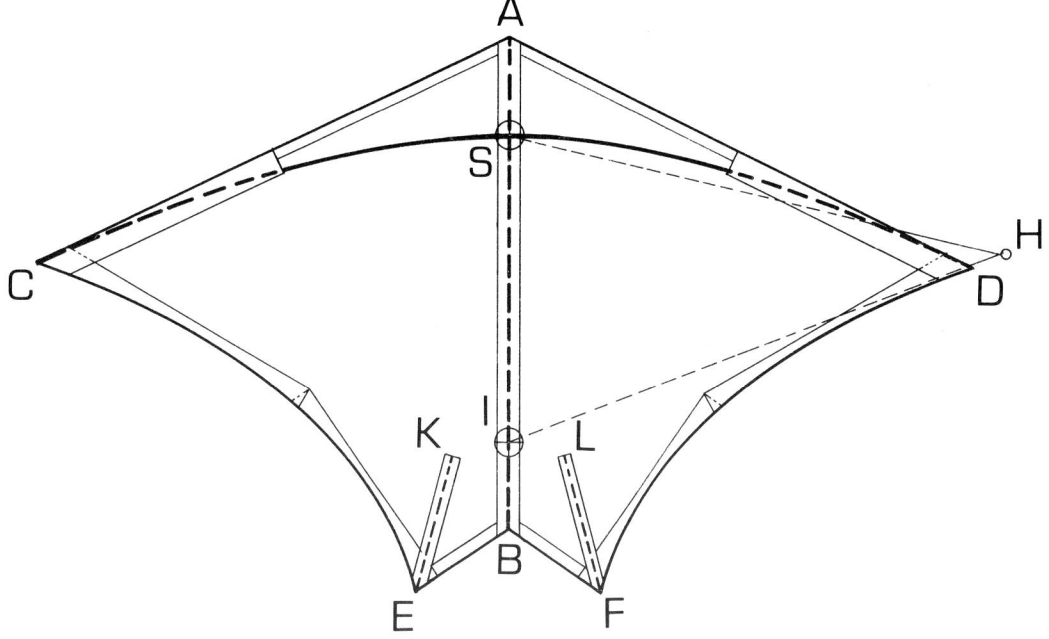

Lawrence's Fighter (Martyn Lawrence)

Martyn Lawrence is an expert fighter kite designer. I met him while travelling in England. This is one of his designs which can be flown by the expert as well as the beginner. This kite is made with spinnaker sail-type material. The cover could also be made with paper or other material. Martyn and I spent a long weekend trying out all his designs, as well as some of Mr. Takeshi Nishibayashi's.

107 *Lawrence's Fighter*

Construction

Length   AB = 47cm (18³/₄in)

Width   CD = 53cm (21¹/₄in)

Sides   AC–AD = 33cm (13¹/₄in)
          CB–DB = 37·5cm (15in)

Bow   CSD = 59cm (23¹/₂in)

Double bow   21cm (8¹/₄in)

Bridle system   SH = 27·5cm (11in)
                  IH = 32cm (12³/₄in)
                  AS = 8·5cm (3³/₈in)
                  AI = 37·5cm (15in)

The bow is made with a fibre of 2mm (¹/₁₀in) and the extra piece for the double bow system is also a fibre of 2mm (¹/₁₀in). It is reinforced with an extra piece of fibre to make it stronger. This increases the speed of the kite. If you are aiming to build a beginner's kite, use just one fibre.

Martyn has built his kite so that it can be dismantled, which is why his bow is attached to the kite with a small string which is permanently fixed on the central stick at S.

The central stick is a split bamboo of 3mm (¹/₈in) and shaped in a curve to give more 'body' to the kite keel.

Reinforce both the tail and the front of the kite. If you use material which will need to be stitched, make small pockets to house the ends of the bow.

108 *Lawrence's Fighter construction diagram*

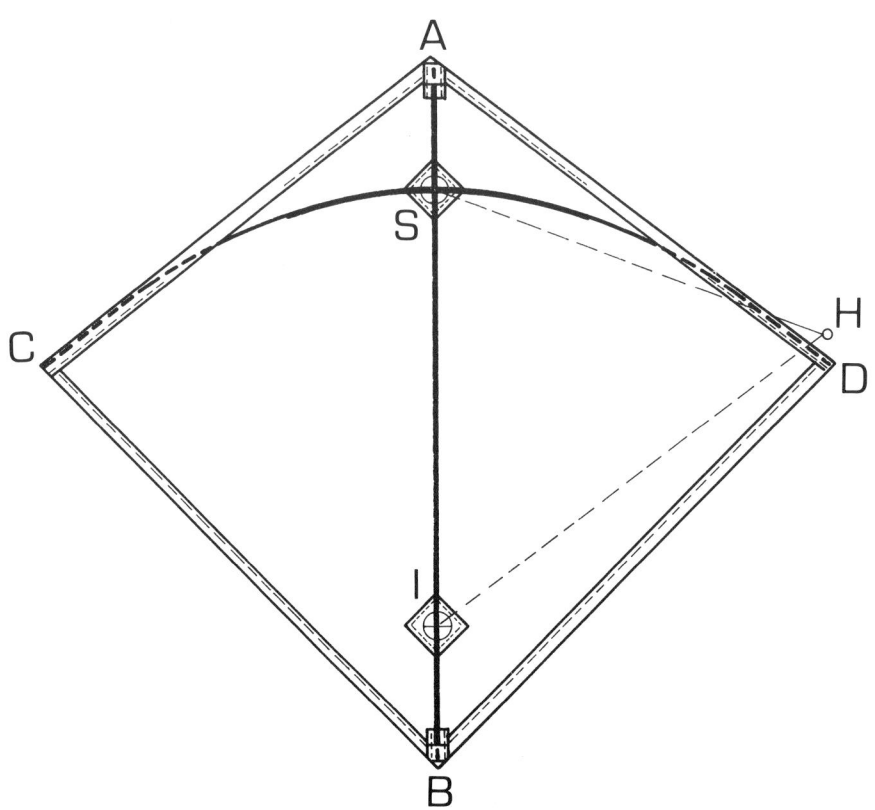

The Indian Star (or Afghan Fighter) Kite (Tony Slater)

I am afraid that I have not been able to find out who was the original designer of the Indian Star kite. This one is a version by Tony Slater.

The shape of this kite is unusual. The flight also has a different 'feel' compared with the more 'traditional' shape. Enjoy flying this kite for its appearance and its way of moving about in the sky.

I think that building this model needs more experience, so I suggest that you only build it after attempting a few simpler constructions.

109 *A member of the Indian team with his Indian Star*

110 *The author's Indian Star*

Construction

Lay down a thin sheet of plastic or opened plastic bag, stick it to a board and start working. Your first job is to draw the kite on the cover. Draw the lines for the sticks, as this will guide you to place each one in the correct position, the longest stick being the first one to be put into place. As the kite is built with thin plastic, it will only take tape to fix the different parts.

Length   AB = 50cm (20in)

Width   CD = 50cm (20in)

Sticks or cross spars   AOB = 50cm (20in)
OC–OD = 25cm (10in)
OF–OF′–OL–OL′–OM–OM′ = 32·5cm (13in)
OE–OE′ = 24cm (11$^3/_4$in)

Sides   AE–AE′ = 13cm (5$^1/_4$in)
FC–F′D = 13cm (5$^1/_4$in)
ML–M′L′ = 12cm (4$^3/_4$in)
EF–E′F′ = 12cm (4$^3/_4$in)
BM–BM′ = 13·5cm (5$^3/_8$in)

Bridle system   AS = 6·5cm (2$^1/_2$in)
IB = 13cm (5$^1/_4$in)
SH = 34·5cm (13$^3/_4$in)
IH = 37·5cm (15in)

Bow   CSD = 66cm (26$^3/_8$in)

111 *Indian Star
construction diagram*

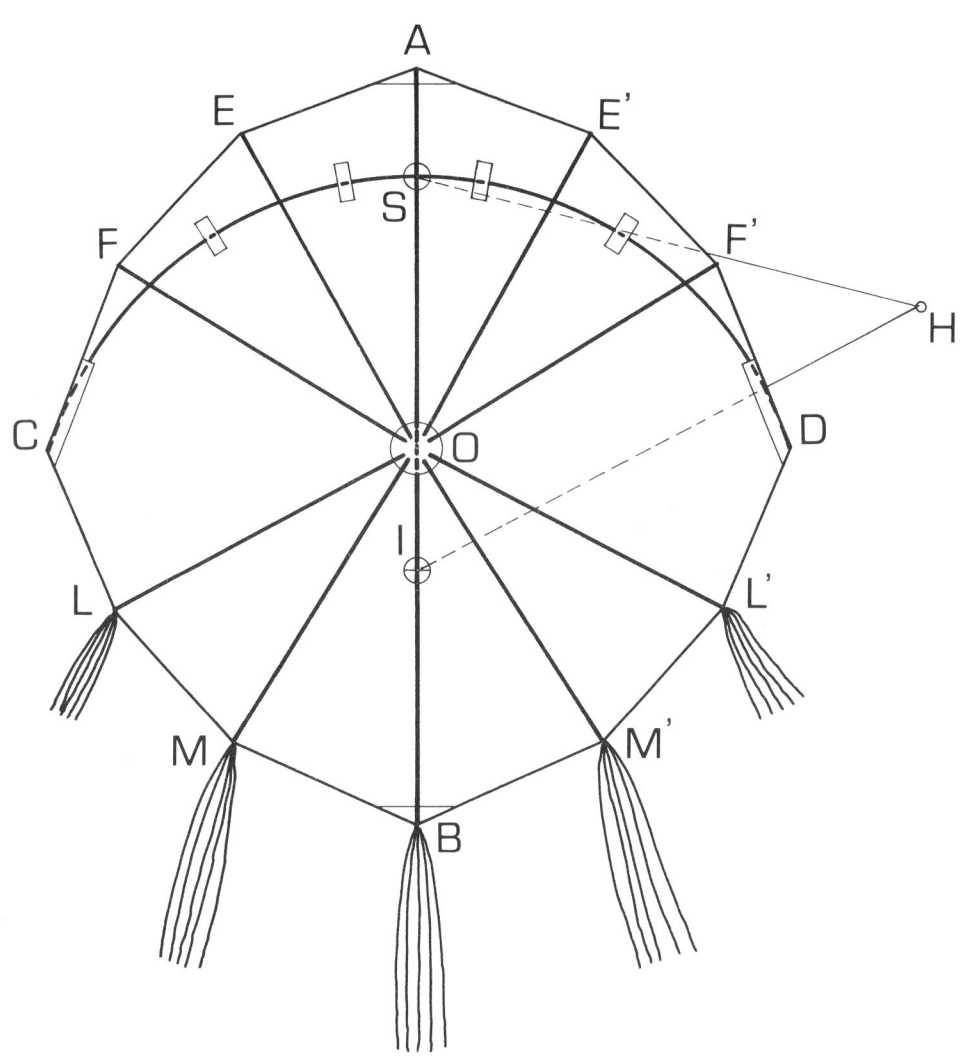

The bow is a 2mm ($^{1}/_{10}$in) fibre and is fixed with extra tape at the tips. It should be added once all the sticks have been taped to the cover. A small piece of tape will maintain the bow in between the spars.

All the sticks are made of split bamboo of 4mm ($^{3}/_{16}$in) $\times$ 2mm ($^{1}/_{10}$in) and taped to the cover. The central point of the kite is a cut piece of carpet tape which keeps all the spars stuck together.

The tail pieces are made with coloured plastic and are attached to the spars.

For decoration, test your colours beforehand on a spare piece of plastic. A coat of car spray-paint will work, but it doesn't last very long!

Lucy Edward's Little Black Bird

(Philippe Gallot)

One year, during my holidays, I set out to build a new model with a different bow system. The result was this kite, which is a good fighter for beginners. It may take a little more time to make, but it looks lovely in the sky and behaves very well. This kite is dedicated to my children, who spent some time helping me to construct the first model!

The cover of the kite is made from a plastic bag, reinforced all around with tape. You could also use paper or some other type of light material. The central stick is of split bamboo, and the spars and bows are made with 2mm ($^{1}/_{10}$in) fibre.

112 *Lucy Edward's Black Bird*

Construction

Length   AB = 38cm (15$^1/_4$in)

Width   CD = 67cm (26$^3/_4$in)

Sides   AE–AF = 24cm (9$^3/_4$in)
EC–FD = 26cm (10$^3/_8$in)
BE–BF = 32cm (12$^3/_4$in)
FV–ET = 19cm (7$^1/_2$in)
CS–DS = 40cm (16in)
AC–AD = 48cm (19$^1/_4$in)
An extra spar is added to strengthen the bows:
TV = 38cm (15$^1/_4$in)

Bridle system   AJ = 8cm (3$^1/_4$in)
IJ = 24cm (9$^3/_4$in)
IH = 38cm (15$^1/_4$in)
JH = 37cm (14$^3/_4$in)

In order to achieve a very fine bow system I have used a 2mm ($^1/_{10}$in) fibre which has been trimmed to 1mm ($^1/_{16}$in) towards the tip of each wing. To do a proper job with a fibre rod, use a very fine file or some fine sand paper. The bows are held in place with a little bit of glue and covered with tape to give a good hold over the plastic.

The central stick must be laid on the cover first. Glue and tape over it. The stick is a split bamboo 4mm ($^3/_{16}$in) × 2mm ($^1/_{10}$in) thick. It must be flexible to give a natural keel shape to the spine of the kite. To keep the bows in place, glue and tape them. While the work is in progress I use a clothes peg to keep each end in the right position.

Fixing the bridle should be the last bit of work. You may now go to the field and enjoy flying your model.

113 *Lucy Edward's Black Bird construction diagram*

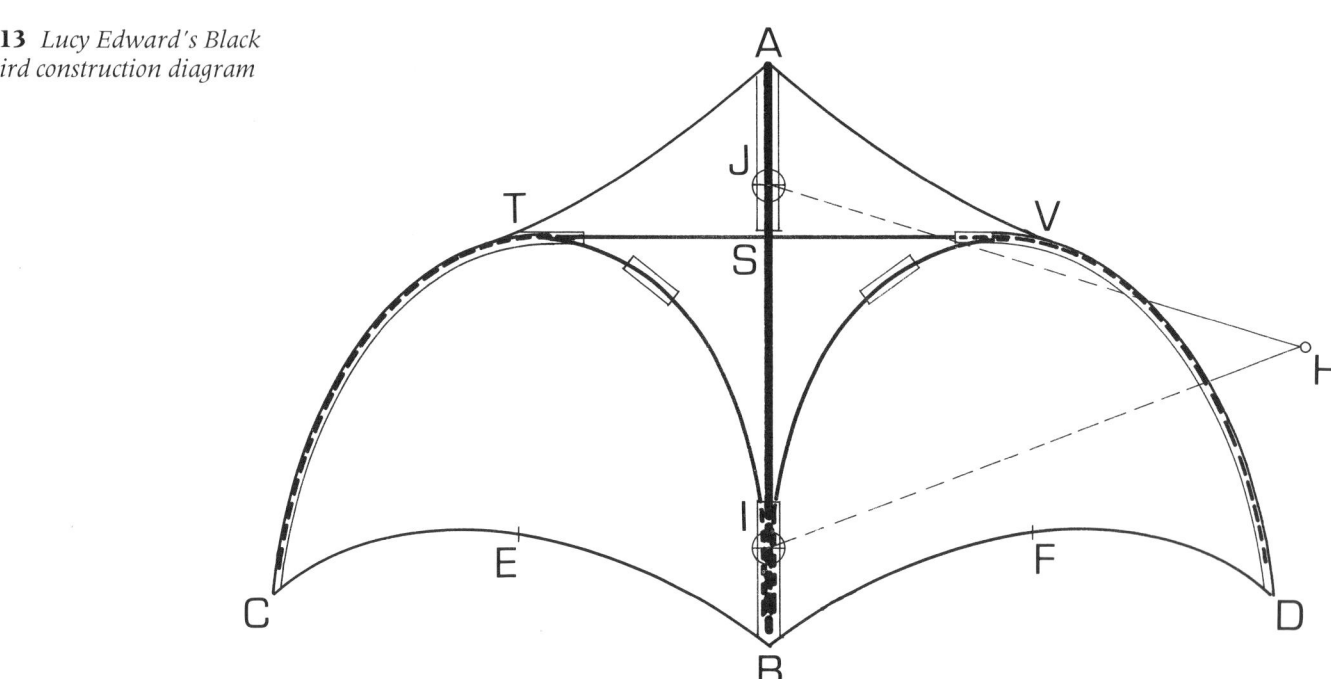

Chapter 9
Mini Fighter Kites

This part of the book is for horrible wet days.

What to do today? Start making mini fighter kites. (We are talking about kites of a maximum width of 20cm (8in)). You may take some of the designs in this book and reduce their size.

For mini fighters, the bamboo bow and sticks have to be really fine. The wind for your flight could be provided by a fan, a ventilator, or by your moving around, playing with the line. The cover can only be made of very fine material – thin plastic, fine paper or very soft Mylar. For this type of kite, use a line made of sewing thread. The bridle points and adjustments will have to be altered to suit the conditions.

On very light breezy days, I play with my mini fighters. When you are away on a trip ... while waiting for a friend ... pull a mini fighter out of your magic bag and have a go! If your front garden is so small that no one would think of flying a kite there ... try your latest mini fighter.

Remember that the mini kite is designed to fly in very special circumstances. Therefore it would not be a good idea to test fly one in a force 10 gale!

I have even seen mini fighters stored in a big matchbox and flown during a kite festival dinner! There are also special indoor championships organised in gymnasiums. Try to join in: it's very exciting!

114 *Mini fighters*

Chapter 10
Making the kite box

You will find that the transport of your fighter kites needs some special attention. I have had several unfortunate trips to the flying field where my kites have been trodden on or damaged while resting on the ground. The best way to protect your work is to use a kite box. Some fighter pilots like to carry their kites in big folders, but I have found that if the kites are kept lying flat and not too squashed, they have a much longer life.

In my kite box I keep several spools for different types of kite, as well as replacement string in case I am cut! A repair kit is also useful: I have several types of tape to repair the cover as well as some glue, a few sticks and some fibre, a few ready-made bows to replace broken ones, and some paper to make a note of addresses of new pilots. Do not forget to put in a pencil too!

My box is rather large, but it was made to fit my largest fighter. You should design your kite box to suit your own needs. The one I suggest here is a copy of mine. When the weather is wet the box will keep your paper kites dry and in good shape. The ground and the grass always collect dew, which causes a lot of

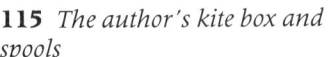
115 *The author's kite box and spools*

damage to fragile kites. If you fly using a bamboo bow, humidity can change its quality and therefore diminish the performance of your fighter kite.

Construction

Length   80cm (32in)

Width   60cm (24in)

Lid height   3·5cm (1³/₈in)

Box height   15cm (6in)

Separation height   12cm (4³/₄in)

Use 6mm (¹/₄in)–8mm (⁵/₁₆in) plywood. Make two parts, the lid and the box. Both parts will be joined with three hinges and the box will have a handle screwed to it. The internal separation is for the spools and repair kit. A coat of paint or varnish will protect the finished box. You may wish to impress by decorating the lid!

This is your safe and your showroom. Make it nice and strong, specially to withstand big feet! Try your biggest fighter kite for the correct measurement; adjust the length and width accordingly.

116 *Kite box construction diagram*

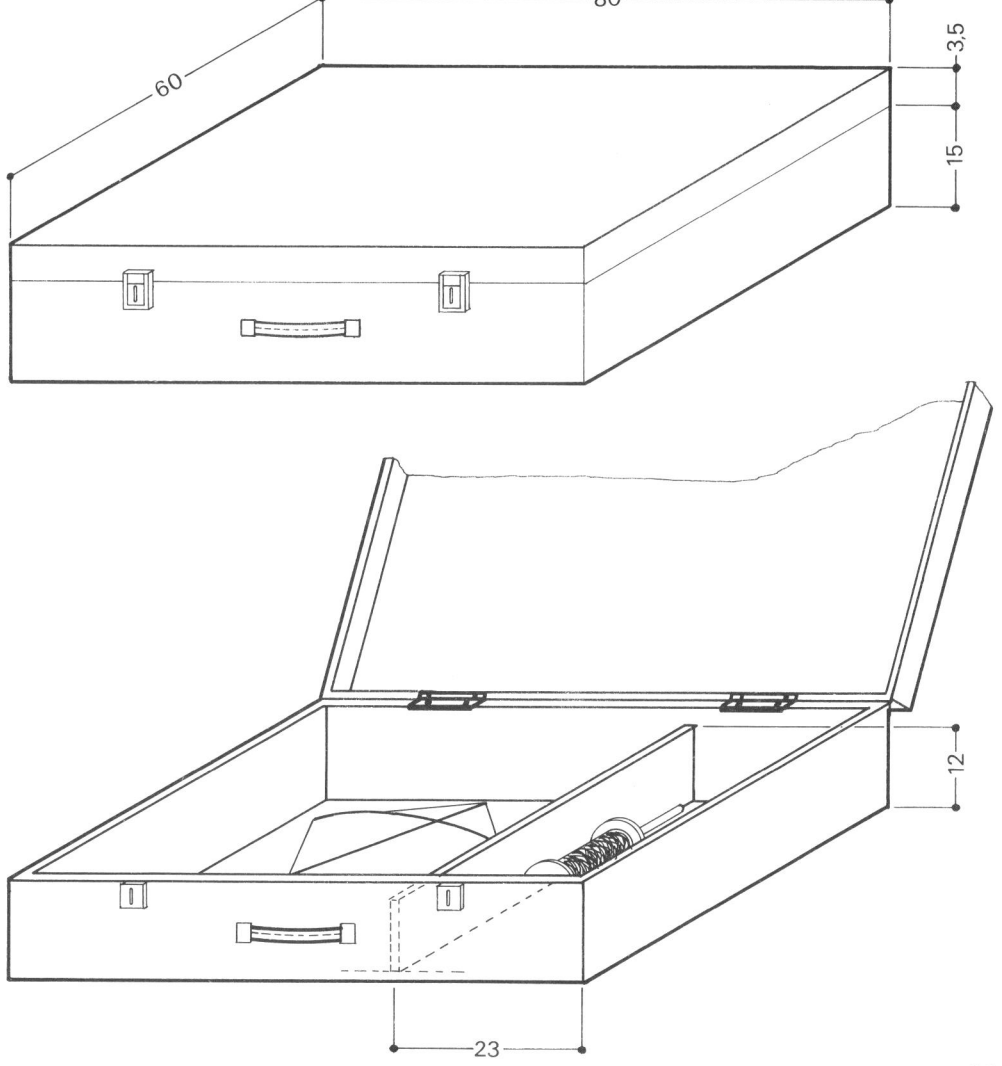

Chapter 11
Games

A fighter kite has other functions apart from fighting. The kite itself, being balanced on its centre of gravity, allows all sorts of tricks. If flown correctly, with experience and technique, just flying a fighter kite is a sport. Visual judgement, as well as hand-eye co-ordination and the control of the line, will give you many hours of relaxation.

Not long ago, I met Joe Vaughan from the United States who is a specialist in Grand Master Fighter Kites. He has made several demonstrations of fighter flying accompanied by music. The kite was actually engaged in a sort of ballet. His performance was superb. I should mention that this show took place indoors!

We have been changing rules for several competitions, due to the fact that, were we to fly amongst spectators, a real fight would be too dangerous. We therefore attached several balloons to a big kite and set the hoard of fighter kites up to pop the balloons. Not easy, but great fun. It demands some expertise, especially when flying with many other pilots at the same time. You can imagine the crossed lines!

Another game is 'follow the leader'. One fighter starts and the rest of the pilots try to follow the same path.

Here are some more possibilities:
- targets towed behind a big kite
- the best low flyer
- the straightest dive and stall
- you may organize a competition where a set of figures has to be completed, e.g. loops, dives, right-angle turns, left turns, vertical figures of eight, horizontal figures of eight, zig-zag vertical flight
- a small, very light paper tail, attached to one kite, to be cut off by other fighters
- trying to land on top of a big kite
- knocking off a plastic bottle placed on top of a pole
- flying through obstacles
- if there is no wind, try to be the longest in the air ... every trick is permitted.

I am sure that you will be able to invent your own games!

Chapter 12
A final word ...

There is no doubt that this book is not complete, nor have I covered every aspect of the world's fighter kites. I do not claim to be a superstar in the field of fighter kites, and I certainly would not pretend to know it all!

The aim of this book is to offer many different designs by my friends and myself, in order to share our enthusiasm and our hobby time with many other fighter kite constructors-to-be. We all seek new shapes, new ideas and new models to build. This attempt hopes to satisfy the few who have experimented

117 *The author holding two spools loaded with cutting line. The kite is one of Tony Slater's Butterflies*

with this type of kite, and encourage the majority to get building a new type of kite.

Nowadays, it seems that a boom in flying double-line directional kites is taking place. Maybe we are forgetting that a single-line controlled fighter kite is also very attractive to manipulate.

I remain modest but happy to have undertaken this exercise; I do hope that I have achieved my goals and will have the great pleasure of seeing some of my designs in the sky …

This would be the best reward for my efforts.

119 *Martyn Lawrence checking the final fine adjustment for his homemade design*

118 *The author is here covering his fingers with tape to protect them during the fight. Cutting line, even when used with expertise, can cause severe cuts*

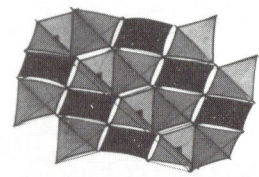

120 *A fighter attacks several balloons towed by a large kite. The aim of the game is to burst the balloon. The large kite is one of Mr Cassagne's latest models.*

Further reading

David Pelham, *The Penguin Book of Kites*, Penguin (This book is my kite Bible!)

Lee Scott Newman and Jay Hartly Newman, *Le Livre des Cerf-volants* (translated by Andre d'Allemagne), L'Etincelle (first published by Kitecraft)

W. Schimmelpfennig, *Making and Flying Kites,* Hamlyn

Jim Rowlands, *Making and Flying Modern Kites,* Dryad Press (no fighters, but several fighter designers are mentioned. A good book for other types of kite)

Dinesh Bahadur, *Come Fight a Kite* (O.P. As far as I know, the only book to deal specifically with fighters.)

Kite Lines, an American magazine, is a must for kiters, and often has excellent articles on fighter kites.

Try to contact your local kite club and ask for their newsletter.

Index